TO THE MOON

Also by Carol Ann Duffy in Picador

The World's Wife

Feminine Gospels

New Selected Poems 1984–2004

Rapture

AS EDITOR

Hand in Hand

Answering Back

TO
THE
MOON

An Anthology of Lunar Poems

Edited by

CAROL ANN
DUFFY

PICADOR

First published 2009 by Picador
an imprint of Pan Macmillan Ltd
Pan Macmillan, 20 New Wharf Road, London N1 9RR
Basingstoke and Oxford
Associated companies throughout the world
www.panmacmillan.com

ISBN 978-0-330-46131-3

1 3 5 7 9 8 6 4 2

A CIP catalogue record for this book is available from
the British Library.

Printed in the UK by CPI Mackays, Chatham ME5 8TD

for Helen Taylor

and Michael Woods

with love

Hey diddle diddle,
the cat and the fiddle,
the cow jumped over the moon.
The little dog laughed
to see such sport
and the dish ran away with the spoon.

'I want a lump in his throat to obstruct the wisecrack.'

VLADIMIR NABOKOV (1899–1977) on being asked what he would like to hear
an astronaut say when landing on the moon for the first time

'Don't let's ask for the moon – we have the stars.'

BETTE DAVIS as Charlotte Vale in the film *Now, Voyager*

Contents

Introduction

From the 'silver face' of Sappho's moon to the 'pert peering creature' of Alice Oswald's, the moon has always been, and always will be, the supremely prized image for poets – a mirror to reflect the poetic imagination; language's human smile against death's darkness. As the twelfth-century Japanese poet Kojiju wrote:

> Merely to know
> The Flawless Moon dwells pure
> In the human heart
> Is to find the Darkness of the night
> Vanished under clearing skies.

I began to assemble this anthology of lunar poems after editing *Answering Back*, in which living poets replied to poems from the past. I was astonished to see how many of those poems, though crossing centuries, referred, above all, to the moon. Although there are well over one hundred poems in *To the Moon*, there could easily have been double or treble that amount and I hope that the reader who enjoys the selection here will, over time, slip their own choices between its pages: moon scraps. The best anthologist, after all, is the reader of poetry. The earliest poem here was written around 600 BC, the latest in our own twenty-first century, and there is something intensely moving in the recurring picture of the poet, the pen, the poem, the constant moon, over what suddenly seems a vulnerably short span of time. We move, for example, from Sappho's girls dancing under the 'low full moon' to Archibald MacLeish's 'Voyage to the Moon' in only eighty poems – poems written in exile, in love, in despair, in wartime, in wonder and enquiry, in all our human conditions. What we have here, as Thomas Hardy writes in 'To the Moon', is 'the human tune'. Tu Fu sang it in the eighth century just as marvellously as the Poet Laureate Ted Hughes did in the twentieth.

When astronauts from the USA first landed and walked on the surface of the moon, forty years ago on 21 July 1969, not every poet was best pleased at the playing of golf and the planting of the Stars and Stripes on such a poetically sacred symbol. To some, it seemed like a trespass of the imagination itself. 'Unsmudged, thank God,' wrote W. H. Auden, 'My Moon still queens the heavens' – that 'my' revealing the poet's possessiveness of the earth's smitten satellite. Since then, of course, science and poetry are closer, more mutually sympathetic, and poets are already seeking new ways, through dialogue with scientists, to respond to the awesome ecological challenges of this century.

The unifying theme of *To the Moon* gives us a real sense of our time on this planet. Poems from centuries past gain freshness, as though they were only written yesterday, and show us not only our distance from, but our closeness to the past:

I climbed the hill just as the new moon showed,
I saw him coming on the southern road.
My heart lays down its load.

These lines from the *Chinese Book of Odes*, written around 500 BC, measure also our distance from, and closeness to, the moon. In doing so, they reveal to us, like all the poems here, how much we share and have shared on this planet we inhabit. Poetry, like the moon itself, sheds a unique light on our lives on this earth.

The Moon

The Stars about the lovely moon
Fade back and vanish very soon,
When, round and full, her silver face
Swims into sight, and lights all space.

Sappho (c. 610–570 bc)

Translated by Edwin Arnold

Full Moon

Off in the twilight hung the low full moon,
And all the women stood before it grave,
As round an altar. Thus at holy times
The Cretan damsels dance melodiously
With delicate feet about the sacrifice,
Trampling the tender bloom of the soft grass.

SAPPHO (c. 610–570 BC)

Translated by William Ellery Leonard

The Morning Glory

The morning glory climbs above my head,
Pale flowers of white and purple, blue and red.
I am disquieted.

Down in the withered grasses something stirred;
I thought it was his footfall that I heard.
Then a grasshopper chirred.

I climbed the hill just as the new moon showed,
I saw him coming on the southern road.
My heart lays down its load.

from the *Shi King* or *Book of Odes*, compiled c. 500 BC

Translated by Helen Waddell

Flowers and Moonlight
on the Spring River

The evening river is level and motionless –
The spring colours just open to their full.
Suddenly a wave carries the moon away
And the tidal water comes with its freight of stars.

YANG-TI (569–618)

Translated by Arthur Waley

Full Moon

Isolate and full, the moon
Floats over the house by the river.
Into the night the cold water rushes away below the gate.
The bright gold spilled on the river is never still.
The brilliance of my quilt is greater than precious silk.
The circle without blemish.
The empty mountains without sound.
The moon hangs in the vacant, wide constellations.
Pine cones drop in the old garden.
The senna trees bloom.
The same clear glory extends for ten thousand miles.

TU FU (712–770)

Translated by Kenneth Rexroth

Moonlit Night

In Fuzhou, far away, my wife is watching
The moon alone tonight, and my thoughts fill
With sadness for my children, who can't think
Of me here in Changan; they're too young still.
Her cloud-soft hair is moist with fragrant mist.
In the clear light her white arms sense the chill.
When will we feel the moonlight dry our tears,
Leaning together on our window-sill?

TU FU (712–770)

Translated by Vikram Seth

Living in the Summer Mountains

I have moved to this home of Immortals.
Wild shrubs bloom everywhere.
In the front garden, trees
Spread their branches for clothes racks.
I sit on a mat and float wine cups
In the cool spring.
Beyond the window railing
A hidden path leads away
Into the dense bamboo grove.
In a gauze dress
I read among my disordered
Piles of books.
I take a leisurely ride
In the painted boat,
And chant poems to the moon.
I drift at ease, for I know
The soft wind will blow me home.

YU HSUAN-CHI (843–868)

Translated by Kenneth Rexroth and Ling Chung

Riddle

A curious and wonderful creature I saw,
– bright air-grail, brave artefact –
homing from a raid with its haul of silver
brimming precarious crescent horns.

To build itself a hideaway up in the city,
a room in a tower, timbered with art,
was all it aimed at, if only it might.

Then over the wall rose a wonder familiar
to the earth race, to everyone known.
It gathered to itself the hoard, and to its home drove off
that unhappy outcast. Onward it coursed,
wandered westward with wasting heart.

Dust rose to the skies, dew fell to the earth,
night was no more. No man knew
along what ways it wandered after.

ANON. (c. 960)

Translated by Michael Alexander

Although the Wind

Although the wind
blows terribly here,
the moonlight also leaks
between the roof planks
of this ruined house.

LADY IZUMI SHIKIBU (c. 970–1030)

Translated by Jane Hirshfield and Mariko Aratani

Moon, Flowers, Man

I raise my cup and invite
The moon to come down from the
Sky. I hope she will accept
Me. I raise my cup and ask
The branches, heavy with flowers,
To drink with me. I wish them
Long life and promise never
To pick them. In company
With the moon and the flowers,
I get drunk, and none of us
Ever worries about good
Or bad. How many people
Can comprehend our joy? I
Have wine and moon and flowers.
Who else do I want for drinking companions?

SU TUNG-P'O (1036–1101)

Translated by Kenneth Rexroth

On the Spirit of the Heart
as Moon-Disk

Merely to know
The Flawless Moon dwells pure
In the human heart
Is to find the Darkness of the night
Vanished under clearing skies.

KOJIJU (1121–1201)

Translated by Edwin A. Cranston

Night Thoughts

I cannot sleep. The long, long
Night is full of bitterness.
I sit alone in my room,
Beside a smoky lamp.
I rub my heavy eyelids
And idly turn the pages
Of my book. Again and again
I trim my brush and stir the ink.
The hours go by. The moon comes
In the open window, pale
And bright like new money.
At last I fall asleep and
I dream of the days on the
River at Tsa-feng, and the
Friends of my youth in Yen Chao.
Young and happy we ran
Over the beautiful hills.
And now the years have gone by,
And I have never gone back.

LU YU (1125–1209)

Translated by Kenneth Rexroth

Evening on the Mountain:
Song to the Moon in a Well

1.

Blue water ripples the well at the corner of the mossy rock.
The new moon is beautifully etched therein.
I scoop out some water but only half a shadow enters my jar.
I fear I'll bring only half the golden mirror home.

2.

A mountain monk coveted the moon;
he drew water, a whole jar full;
but when he reached his temple, he discovered
that tilting the jar meant spilling the moon.

YI KYUBO (1168–1241)

Translated by Kevin O'Rourke

The Neglected Wife

One moon of joy I knew,
And in the waning radiance of that moon
I gave you a folding fan.

Your love was lighter than the fragrant wind
Stirred by these sticks of carven sandalwood.

The moon sank down behind the city wall.
How bitter was the wine we drank at dawn!

Soon came the whisper of a silken shirt.
Soon came the perfume of a jasmine flower.
Swiftly for you there rose another moon.

Your new wife's face is like a jasmine petal
And like a fallen petal it will fade
After the moon goes down.

I think you do not know how cruel you are,
But why was your parting gift to me
Another folding fan?

YI TALCH'UNG (c. 1385)

Translated by Jean S. Grigsby

Mad Song

or, Tom O'Bedlam's Song

From the hag and hungry goblin
That into rags would rend ye,
All the spirits that stand
By the naked man
In the book of moons, defend ye,

That of your five sound senses
You never be forsaken,
Nor wander from
Yourselves with Tom
Abroad to beg your bacon.

With a thought I took for Maudlin,
And a cruse of cockle pottage,
With a thing thus tall,
Sky bless you all,
I befell into this dotage.

I slept not since the Conquest,
Till then I never waked,
Till the roguish boy
Of love where I lay
Me found and stript me naked.

The moon's my constant mistress,
And the lonely owl my marrow;
The flaming drake
And the night-crow make
Me music to my sorrow.

I know more than Apollo,
For oft, when he lies sleeping,
I see the stars
At mortal wars
In the wounded welkin weeping.

The moon embrace her shepherd,
And the queen of love her warrior,
While the first doth horn
The star of morn,
And the next the heavenly farrier.

With an host of furious fancies,
Wherof I am commander,
With a burning spear
And a horse of air
To the wilderness I wander;

By a knight of ghosts and shadows
I summoned am to tourney
Ten leagues beyond
The wide world's end –
Methinks it is no journey.

ANON. (c. 1500)

from *Epithalamion*

Who is the same, which at my window peepes?
Or whose is that faire face, that shines so bright,
Is it not Cinthia, she that never sleepes,
But walkes about high heaven al the night?
O fayrest goddesse, do thou not envy
My love with me to spy:
For thou likewise didst love, though now unthought,
And for a fleece of woll, which privily,
The Latmian shephard once unto thee brought,
His pleasures with thee wrought.
Therefore to us be favorable now;
And sith of wemens labours thou hast charge,
And generation goodly dost enlarge,
Encline thy will t'effect our wishful vow,
And the chast wombe informe with timely seed,
That may our comfort breed:
Till which we cease our hopefull hap to sing,
Ne let the woods us answere, nor our Eccho ring.

EDMUND SPENSER (c. 1552–1599)

from *Astrophil and Stella*

31.

With how sad steps, o Moone, thou climbs't the skies,
How silently, and with how wanne a face,
What, may it be that even in heav'nly place
That busie archer his sharpe arrowes tries?
Sure, if that long with *Love* acquainted eyes
Can judge of *Love*, thou feel'st a Lover's case;
I reade it in thy lookes, thy languisht grace,
To me that feele the like, thy state descries.
Then e'vn of fellowship, o Moone, tell me
Is constant *Love* deem'd there but want of wit?
Are Beauties there as proud as here they be?
Do they above love to be lov'd, and yet
Those Lovers scorne whom that *Love* doth possesse?
Do they call *Vertue* there ungratefulnesse?

SIR PHILIP SIDNEY (1554–1586)

Of the Moon

Look how the pale queen of the silent night
Doth cause the Ocean to attend upon her,
And he, as long as she is in his sight,
With his full tide is ready her to honour;
But when the silver waggon of the Moon
Is mounted up so high he canot follow,
The sea calls home his crystal waves to moan,
And with low ebb doth manifest his sorrow.
So you, that are the sovreign of my heart,
Have all my joys attending on your will,
My joys low-ebbing when you do depart –
When you return, their tide my heart doth fill:
So as you come, and as you do depart,
Joys ebb and flow within my tender heart.

CHARLES BEST (15??–1602)

Hymn to Diana

Queen and Huntress, chaste and fair,
Now the sun is laid to sleep,
Seated in thy silver chair
State in wonted manner keep:
Hesperus entreats thy light,
Goddess excellently bright.

Earth, let not thy envious shade
Dare itself to interpose;
Cynthia's shining orb was made
Heaven to clear when day did close:
Bless us then with wished sight,
Goddess excellently bright.

Lay thy bow of pearl apart
And thy crystal-shining quiver;
Give unto the flying hart
Space to breathe, how short soever:
Thou that mak'st a day of night,
Goddess excellently bright!

BEN JONSON (1574–1637)

Eternitie

O Yeares! and Age! Farewell:
    Behold I go,
    Where I do know
Infinitie to dwell.

And these mine eyes shall see
    All times, how they
    Are lost i' the Sea
Of vast Eternitie.

Where never Moone shall sway
    The Starres; but she
    And Night, shall be
Drown'd in one endlesse Day.

ROBERT HERRICK (1591–1674)

To Music, to Becalm a Sweet
Sick Youth

Charms, that call down the moon from out her sphere,
On this sick youth work your enchantments here!
Bind up his senses with your numbers, so
As to entrance his pain, or cure his woe.
Fall gently, gently, and a-while him keep
Lost in the civil wilderness of sleep:
That done, then let him, dispossess'd of pain,
Like to a slumbering bride, awake again.

ROBERT HERRICK (1591–1674)

Thanks, Gentle Moone, for thy Obscured Light

Thanks, gentle Moone, for thy obscured light;
My love and I betraied thou set us free.
And Zephirus, as many unto thee,
Whose blasts conceald the pleasures of the night;
Resolve to her thou gave, content to mee.
But be those bowers still fild with serpents' hisses,
That sought by treason to betray our kisses.

And thou, false Arbor with thy bed of Rose,
Wherin, wheron, toucht equall with love's fyer,
We reapt of eyther other love's desire,
Wither the twining plants that thee enclose!
Oh be thy bowers still fild with serpents' hisses,
That sought by treason to betray our kisses.

Torne be the frame, for thou did thankless hide
A trayterous spy, her brother and my foe,
Who sought by death our joyes to undergoe,
And by that death our passions to devide,
Leaving to our great vows, eternall woe.
O be thy bowers still fild with serpents' hisses,
That sought by treason to betray our kisses.

ANON. (1605–)

The Nightingale

Sweet bird, that shunn'st the noise of folly,
Most musical, most melancholy!
Thee, chauntress, oft, the woods among,
I woo, to hear thy even-song;
And missing thee, I walk unseen
On the dry, smooth-shaven green,
To behold the wandering moon
Riding high her highest noon,
Like one that had been led astray
Through the heaven's wide pathless way;
And oft, as if her head she bow'd,
Stooping through a fleecy cloud.

JOHN MILTON (1608–1674)

from Book IV of *Paradise Lost*

With thee conversing, I forget all time,
All seasons and thir change, all please alike.
Sweet is the breath of morn, her rising sweet,
With charm of earliest Birds; pleasant the Sun
When first on this delightful Land he spreads
His orient Beams, on herb, tree, fruit, and flow'r,
Glist'ring with dew; fragrant the fertile earth
After soft showers; and sweet the coming on
Of grateful Ev'ning mild, then silent Night
With this her solemn Bird and this fair Moon,
And these the Gems of Heav'n, her starry train:
But neither breath of Morn when she ascends
With charm of earliest Birds, nor rising Sun
On this delightful land, nor herb, fruit, flow'r,
Glist'ring with dew, nor fragrance after showers,
Nor grateful Ev'ning mild, nor silent Night
With this her solemn Bird, nor walk by Moon
Or glittering Star-Light, without thee is sweet.

JOHN MILTON (1608–1674)

To The Moon

Queen of the silver bow! – by thy pale beam,
Alone and pensive, I delight to stray,
And watch thy shadow trembling in the stream,
Or mark the floating clouds that cross thy way.
And while I gaze, thy mild and placid light
Sheds a soft calm upon my troubled breast;
And oft I think – fair planet of the night –
That in thy orb, the wretched may have rest:
The sufferers of the earth perhaps may go,
Released by Death – to thy benignant sphere,
And the sad children of Despair and Woe
Forget, in thee, their cup of sorrow here.
Oh! that I soon may reach thy world serene,
Poor wearied pilgrim – in this toiling scene!

CHARLOTTE SMITH (1749–1806)

Moon

Thee too, modest tressed maid,
When thy fallen stars appear;
When in lawn of fire array'd
Sov'reign of yon powder'd sphere;
To thee I chant at close of day,
Beneath, O maiden Moon! thy ray.

Throned in sapphired ring supreme,
Pregnant with celestial juice,
On silver wing thy diamond stream
Given what summer hours produce;
While view'd impearl'd earth's rich inlay,
Beneath, O maiden Moon! thy ray.

Glad, pale Cynthian wine I sip,
Breathed the flow'ry leaves among;
Draughts delicious wet my lip;
Drown'd in nectar drunk my song;
While tuned to Philomel the lay,
Beneath, O maiden Moon! thy ray.

Dew, that od'rous ointment yields,
Sweets, that western winds disclose,
Bathing spring's more purpled fields,
Soft's the band that winds the rose;
While o'er thy myrtled lawns I stray
Beneath, O maiden Moon! thy ray.

HENRY ROWE (1750–1819)

The Rigs o' Barley

It was upon a Lammas night,
When corn rigs are bonnie,
Beneath the moon's unclouded night,
I held away to Annie;
The time flew by wi' tentless heed
Till 'tween the late and early,
Wi' sma' persuasion, she agreed
To see me thro' the barley.
Corn rigs, an' barley rigs,
An' corn rigs are bonnie:
I'll ne'er forget that happy night,
Amang the rigs wi' Annie.

The sky was blue, the wind was still,
The moon was shining clearly:
I set her doon, wi' right good will,
Amang the rigs o' barley:
I ken't her heart was a' my ain:
I lov'd her most sincerely;
I kiss'd her owre and owre again,
Amang the rigs o' barley.
Corn rigs, an' barley rigs,
An' corn rigs are bonnie:
I'll ne'er forget that happy night,
Amang the rigs wi' Annie.

I lock'd her in my fond embrace;
Her heart was beating rarely:
My blessings on that happy place,
Amang the rigs o' barley!
But by the moon and stars so bright,
That shone that hour so clearly!
She aye shall bless that happy night,
Amang the rigs o' barley.
Corn rigs, an' barley rigs,
An' corn rigs are bonnie:
I'll ne'er forget that happy night,
Amang the rigs wi' Annie.

I ha'e been blythe wi' comrades dear;
I ha'e been merry drinkin';
I ha'e been joyful gatherin' gear;
I ha'e been happy thinkin':
But a' the pleasures e'er I saw,
Tho' three times doubled fairly,
That happy night was worth them a',
Amang the rigs o' barley.
Corn rigs an' barley rigs,
An' corn rigs are bonnie:
I'll ne'er forget that happy night,
Amang the rigs wi' Annie.

ROBERT BURNS (1759–1796)

Frost at Midnight

The Frost performs its secret ministry,
Unhelped by any wind. The owlet's cry
Came loud – and hark, again! loud as before.
The inmates of my cottage, all at rest,
Have left me to that solitude, which suits
Abstruser musings: save that at my side
My cradled infant slumbers peacefully.
'Tis calm indeed! so calm, that it disturbs
And vexes meditation with its strange
And extreme silentness. Sea, hill and wood,
This populous village! Sea, and hill, and wood,
With all the numberless goings-on of life,
Inaudible as dreams! the thin blue flame
Lies on my low-burnt fire, and quivers not;
Only that film, which fluttered on the grate,
Still flutters there, the sole unquiet thing.
Methinks, its motion in this hush of nature
Gives it dim sympathies with me who live,
Making it a companionable form,
Whose puny flaps and freaks the idling Spirit
By its own moods interprets, every where
Echo or mirror seeking of itself,
And makes a toy of Thought.

                                        But O! how oft,
How oft, at school, with most believing mind,
Presageful, have I gazed upon the bars,
To watch that fluttering *stranger*! and as oft
With unclosed lids, already had I dreamt
Of my sweet birth-place, and the old church-tower,
Whose bells, the poor man's only music, rang
From morn to evening, all the hot Fair-day,
So sweetly, that they stirred and haunted me
With a wild pleasure, falling on mine ear
Most like articulate sounds of things to come!
So gazed I, till the soothing things, I dreamt,
Lulled me to sleep, and sleep prolonged my dreams!
And so I brooded all the following morn,
Awed by the stern preceptor's face, mine eye
Fixed with mock study on my swimming book:
Save if the door half opened, and I snatched
A hasty glance, and still my heart leaped up,
For still I hoped to see the *stranger's* face,
Townsman, or aunt, or sister more beloved,
My play-mate when we both were clothed alike!

Dear Babe, that sleepest cradled by my side,
Whose gentle breathings, heard in this deep calm,
Fill up the interspersed vacancies
And momentary pauses of the thought!
My babe so beautiful! it thrills my heart
With tender gladness, thus to look at thee,
And think that thou shalt learn far other lore,
And in far other scenes! For I was reared
In the great city, pent 'mid cloisters dim,
And saw nought lovely but the sky and stars.
But *thou*, my babe! shalt wander like a breeze
By lakes and sandy shores, beneath the crags
Of ancient mountain, and beneath the clouds,
Which image in their bulk both lakes and shores
And mountain crags: so shalt thou see and hear
The lovely shapes and sounds intelligible
Of that eternal language, which thy God
Utters, who from eternity doth teach
Himself in all, and all things in himself.
Great universal teacher! he shall mould
Thy spirit, and by giving make it ask.

Therefore all seasons shall be sweet to thee,
Whether the summer clothe the general earth
With greeness, or the redbreast sit and sing
Betwixt the tufts of snow on the bare branch
Of mossy apple-tree, while the nigh thatch
Smokes in the sun-thaw; whether the eave-drops fall
Heard only in the trances of the blast,
Or if the secret ministry of frost
Shall hang them up in silent icicles,
Quietly shining to the quiet Moon.

S. T. COLERIDGE (1772–1834)

A Soliloquy of the Full Moon, She Being in a Mad Passion

Now as Heaven is my Lot, they're the Pests of the Nation!
Wherever they can come
With clankum and blankum
'Tis all Botheration, & Hell & Damnation,
With fun, jeering,
Conjuring,
Sky-staring,
Loungering,
And still to the tune of Transmogrification –
Those muttering
Spluttering
Ventriloquogusty
Poets
With no Hats
Or Hats that are rusty.
They're my Torment and Curse
And harass me worse
And bait me and bay me, far sorer I vow
Than the Screech of the Owl
Or the witch-wolf's long howl,
Or sheep-killing Butcher-dog's inward Bow wow
For me they all spite – an unfortunate Wight.

And the very first moment that I came to Light
A Rascal call'd Voss the more to his scandal,
Turn'd me into a sickle with never a handle.
A Night or two after a worse Rogue there came,
The head of the Gang, one Wordsworth by name –
'Ho! What's in the wind?' 'Tis the voice of a Wizzard!
I saw him look at me most terribly blue!
He was hunting for witch-rhymes from great A to Izzard,
And soon as he'd found them made no more ado
But chang'd me at once to a little Canoe.
From this strange Enchantment uncharm'd by degrees
I began to take Courage and hop'd for some Ease,
When one Coleridge, a Raff of the self-same Banditti
Past by – & intending no doubt to be witty,
Because I'd th' ill-fortune his taste to displease,
He turn'd up his nose,
And in pitiful Prose
Made me into the half of a small Cheshire Cheese.
Well, a night or two past – it was wind, rain & hail –
And I ventur'd abroad in a thick Cloak & veil –
But the very first Evening he saw me again
The last mentioned Ruffian popp'd out of his Den –

I was resting a moment on the bare edge of Naddle
I fancy the sight of me turn'd his Brains addle –
For what was I now?
A complete Barley-mow
And when I clim'd higher he made a long leg,
And chang'd me at once to an Ostrich's Egg –
But now Heaven be praised in contempt of the Loon,
I am I myself I, the jolly full Moon.
Yet my heart is still fluttering –
For I heard the Rogue muttering –
He was hulking and sulking at the skirt of a Wood
When lightly & brightly on tip-toe I stood
On the long level Line of a motionless Cloud
And ho! what a Skittle-ground! quoth he aloud
And wish'd from his heart nine Nine-pins to see
In brightness and size just proportion'd to me.
So I fear'd from my soul,
That he'd make me a Bowl,
But in spite of his spite
This was more than his might
And still Heaven be prais'd! in contempt of the Loon
I am I myself I, the jolly full Moon.

S. T. COLERIDGE (1772–1834)

To the Autumnal Moon

Mild Splendour of the various-vested Night!
Mother of wildly-working visions! hail!
I watch thy gliding, while with watery light
Thy weak eye glimmers through a fleecy veil;
And when thou lovest thy pale orb to shroud
Behind the gather'd blackness lost on high;
And when thou dartest from the wind-rent cloud
Thy placid lightning o'er the awaken'd sky.

Ah such is Hope! as changeful and as fair!
Now dimly peering on the wistful sight;
Now hid behind the dragon-wing'd Despair:
But soon emerging in her radiant might
She o'er the sorrow-clouded breast of Care
Sails, like a meteor kindling in its flight.

S. T. COLERIDGE (1772–1834)

The Young May Moon

The young May moon is beaming, love,
The glow-worm's lamp is gleaming, love;
How sweet to rove
through Morna's grove,
When the drowsy world is dreaming, love!
Then awake! – the heavens look bright, my dear,
'Tis never too late for delight, my dear,
And the best of all ways
To lengthen our days
Is to steal a few hours from the night, my dear!

Now all the world is sleeping, love,
But the Sage, his star-watch keeping, love,
And I, whose star
More glorious far
Is the eye from that casement peeping, love,
Then awake! – till rise of sun, my dear,
Or in watching the flight
Of bodies of light
He might happen to take thee for one, my dear!

THOMAS MOORE (1779–1852)

While Gazing on the Moon's Light

While gazing on the moon's light,
A moment from her smile I turn'd,
To look at orbs that, more bright,
In lone and distant glory burn'd.
But too far
Each proud star,
For me to feel its warming flame;
Much more dear
That mild sphere,
Which near our planet smiling came;
Thus, Mary, be but thou my own,
While brighter eyes unheeded play,
I'll love those moonlight looks alone
That bless my home and guide my way.

The day had sunk in dim showers,
But midnight now, with lustre meet,
Illumined all the pale flowers,
Like hope upon a mourner's cheek.
I said (while
The moon's smile
Play'd o'er a stream, in dimpling bliss,)
'The moon looks
On many brooks,

The brook can see no moon but this;'
And thus, I thought, our fortunes run,
For many a lover looks to thee,
While oh! I feel there is but one,
One Mary in the world for me.

THOMAS MOORE (1779–1852)

We'll Go No More A-Roving

So we'll go no more a-roving
So late into the night,
Though the heart be still as loving
And the moon be still as bright.

For the sword outwears its sheath,
And the soul wears out the breast,
And the heart must pause to breathe
And love itself have rest.

Though the night was made for loving,
And the day returns too soon,
Yet we'll go no more a-roving
By the light of the moon.

LORD BYRON (1788–1824)

The Moon

Art thou pale for weariness
Of climbing heaven, and gazing on the earth,
Wandering companionless
Among the stars that have a different birth –
And ever-changing, like a joyless eye
That finds no object worth its constancy?

And like a dying lady, lean and pale,
Who totters forth, wrapped in a gauzy veil,
Out of her chamber, led by the insane
And feeble wanderings of her fading brain,
The moon arose up in the murky East,
A white and shapeless mass –

PERCY BYSSHE SHELLEY (1792–1822)

from Pleasures of Spring

. . . The boy ne'er mends his pace but soodles on
Blessing the moonlight when the day is gone
And even dares to pause amid the shade
Of the old ruined castle undismayed
To mark the change – that some few weeks ago
Hid its blank walls in draperies of snow,
Marking in joy on its once naked tower
Snub elders greening and full many a flower
Of bloodwalls glowing with rich tawny streaks
Blushing in beauty from the gaping creeks,
Swathy yet lovely by each zephyr fanned
As the soft cheeks of maidens summer tanned,
Wreaths nature loves round ruin'd brows to bind
From seeds took hither by the birds and wind.
He views those garlands and seems struck the while
That things so abject should be seen to smile,
Oft turning to the moon a wandering eye
That seems to journey with him through the sky,
Moves as he moves and stops as glad the while
To wait its leisure while he climbs a stile.
He walks, it walks and keeps his every pace,
Runs when he runs and glories in the race.
He tries his utmost speed to leave behind
His shining friend, and thinks he beats the wind

For swiftness as he pants and hurries on,
Inly exulting that the race is won,
But spite of every vale and weary hill
He passed and climbed so swift, it followed still
And while he hums over each old tune he loves,
Do as he will it moveth as he moves
Swift as his thoughts. His speed is all in vain.
He turns to look and there it is again,
Plump opposite him, gleaming pale and wan,
As near as when his eager race began.
He thinks on the long ways he left behind
And vain wild notions fill his puzzled mind:
The gossip tales that winter did supply
Urge their faint shadows on his gazing eye,
And the pale shades that cloud the moon so wan
His artless fancies fashion to a man.
Oft he has heard, at night, when toil was done,
Rude tales of giants dwelling in the moon
And this as one of those his mind supplies
That takes his nightly journey through the skies.
So here he stops nor urges speed again,
Deeming a race with giants doubly vain.

JOHN CLARE (1793–1864)

To the Moon

Now that the year has come full circle,
I remember climbing this hill, heartbroken,
To gaze up at the graceful sight of you,
And how you hung then above those woods
As you do tonight, bathing them in brightness.
But at that time your face seemed nothing
But a cloudy shimmering through my tears,
So wretched was the life I led: and lead still . . .
Nothing changes, moon of my delight. Yet
I find pleasure in recollection, in calling back
My season of grief: when one is young,
And hope is a long road, memory
A short one, how welcome then
The remembrance of things past – no matter
How sad, and the heart still grieving

GIACOMO LEOPARDI (1798–1837)

The Morning Moon

'Twas when the op'ning dawn was still,
I took my lonely road, uphill,
Toward the eastern sky, in gloom,
Or touch'd with palest primrose bloom;
And there the moon, at morning break,
Though yet unset, was gleaming weak,
And fresh'ning air began to pass,
All voiceless, over darksome grass,
                Before the sun
                Had yet begun
To dazzle down the morning moon.

By Maycreech hillock lay the cows,
Below the ash-trees' nodding boughs,
And water fell, from block to block
Of mossy stone, down Burncleeve rock,
By poplar-trees that stood, as slim
'S a feather, by the stream's green brim;
And down about the mill, that stood
Half darken'd off below the wood,
                The rambling brook,
                From nook to nook,
Flow'd on below the morning moon.

At mother's house I made a stand,
Where no one stirr'd with foot or hand;
No smoke above the chimney reek'd,
No winch above the well-mouth creak'd;
No casement open'd out, to catch
The air below the eaves of thatch;
Nor down below her cleanly floor
Had open'd back her heavy door;
        And there the catch,
        With fasten'd latch,
Stood close, below the morning moon.

And she, dear soul, so good and kind,
Had holden long, in my young mind,
Of holy thoughts, the highest place
Of honour, for her love and grace.
But now my wife, to heart and sight,
May seem to shine a fuller light;
And as the sun may rise to view,
To dim the moon, from pale to blue,
        My comely bride
        May seem to hide
My mother, now my morning moon.

WILLIAM BARNES (1801–1886)

On the Eclipse of the Moon of October 1865

One little noise of life remained – I heard
The train pause in the distance, then rush by,
Brawling and hushing, like some busy fly
That murmurs and then settles; nothing stirred
Beside. The shadow of our travelling earth
Hung on the silver moon, which mutely went
Through that grand process, without token sent,
Or any sign to call a gazer forth,
Had I not chanced to see: dumb was the vault
Of heaven, and dumb the fields – no zephyr swept
The forest walks, or through the coppice crept;
Nor other sound the stillness did assault,
Save that faint-brawling railway's move and halt;
So perfect was the silence Nature kept.

CHARLES TENNYSON TURNER (1808–1879)

The Owl and the Pussycat

The Owl and the Pussy-cat went to sea
    In a beautiful pea-green boat,
They took some honey, and plenty of money,
    Wrapped up in a five-pound note.
The Owl looked up to the stars above,
    And sang to a small guitar,
"O lovely pussy! O Pussy, my love,
    What a beautiful Pussy you are,
        You are,
        You are!
What a beautiful Pussy you are!"

Pussy said to the Owl, "You elegant fowl!
    How charmingly sweet you sing!
O let us be married! too long we have tarried:
    But what shall we do for a ring?"
They sailed away, for a year and a day,
    To the land where the Bong-Tree grows,
And there in a wood a Piggy-wig stood,
    With a ring at the end of his nose,
        His nose,
        His nose,
With a ring at the end of his nose.

"Dear Pig, are you willing to sell for one shilling
    Your ring?" Said the Piggy, "I will."
So they took it away, and were married next day
    By the Turkey who lives on the hill.
They dined on mince, and slices of quince,
    Which they ate with a runcible spoon;
And hand in hand, on the edge of the sand,
    They danced by the light of the moon,
        The moon,
        The moon,
They danced by the light of the moon.

EDWARD LEAR (1812–1888)

Meeting at Night

The grey sea and the long black land;
And the yellow half-moon large and low;
And the startled little waves that leap
In fiery ringlets from their sleep,
As I gain the cove with pushing prow,
And quench its speed i' the slushy sand.
Then a mile of warm sea-scented beach;
Three fields to cross till a farm appears;
A tap at the pane, the quick sharp scratch
And blue spurt of a lighted match,
And a voice less loud, through its joys and fears,
Than the two hearts beating each to each!

ROBERT BROWNING (1812–1889)

The Road

Faint shines the far moon
Through misty night,
Sad lies the dead field
In the moon's light.
White with frost along
The road without end,
Bare-branched their long line
Birches extend.
Bells tinkle, the team
Swiftly whirls along,
My drowsy driver hums
Softly his song.
Onward I travel
In my crazy cart,
Sadly, pitying
The land of my heart.

Nikolay Platonovich Ogarev (1813–1879)

Translated by P. E. Matheson

Look Down, Fair Moon

Look down, fair moon, and bathe this scene;
Pour softly down night's nimbus floods, on faces ghastly, swollen, purple;
On the dead, on their backs, with their arms toss'd wide,
Pour down your unstinted nimbus, sacred moon.

WALT WHITMAN (1819–1892)

Dirge for Two Veterans

The last sunbeam
Lightly falls from the finish'd Sabbath,
On the pavement here, and there beyond it is looking,
Down a new-made double grave.

Lo, the moon ascending,
Up from the east the silvery round moon,
Beautiful over the house-tops, ghastly, phantom moon,
Immense and silent moon.

I see a sad procession,
And I hear the sound of coming full-key'd bugles,
All the channels of the city streets they're flooding,
As with voices and with tears.

I hear the great drums pounding,
And the small drums steady whirring,
And every blow of the great convulsive drums,
Strikes me through and through.

For the son is brought with the father,
(In the foremost ranks of the fierce assault they fell,
Two veterans son and father dropt together,
And the double grave awaits them.)

Now nearer blow the bugles,
And the drums strike more convulsive,
And the daylight o'er the pavement quite has faded,
And the strong dead-march enwraps me.

In the eastern sky up-buoying,
The sorrowful vast phantom moves illumin'd,
('Tis some mother's large transparent face,
In heaven brighter growing.)

O strong dead-march you please me!
O moon immense with your silvery face you soothe me!
O my soldiers twain! O my veterans passing to burial!
What I have I also give you.

The moon gives you light,
And the bugles and the drums give you music,
And my heart, O my soldiers, my veterans,
My heart gives you love.

WALT WHITMAN (1819–1892)

Dover Beach

The sea is calm tonight,
The tide is full, the moon lies fair
Upon the straits; – on the French coast the light
Gleams and is gone; the cliffs of England stand,
Glimmering and vast, out in the tranquil bay.
Come to the window, sweet is the night-air!
Only, from the long line of spray
Where the sea meets the moon-blanched land,
Listen! you hear the grating roar
Of pebbles which the waves draw back, and fling,
At their return, up the high strand,
Begin, and cease, and then again begin,
With tremulous cadence slow, and bring
The eternal note of sadness in.

Sophocles long ago
Heard it on the Ægean, and it brought
Into his mind the turbid ebb and flow
Of human misery; we
Find also in the sound a thought,
Hearing it by this distant northern sea.
The sea of faith
Was once, too, at the full, and round earth's shore
Lay like the folds of a bright girdle furled.

But now I only hear
Its melancholy, long, withdrawing roar,
Retreating, to the breath
Of the night-wind, down the vast edges drear
And naked shingles of the world.

Ah, love, let us be true
To one another! for the world, which seems
To lie before us like a land of dreams,
So various, so beautiful, so new,
Hath really neither joy, nor love, nor light,
Nor certitude, nor peace, nor help for pain;
And we are here as on a darkling plain
Swept with confused alarms of struggle and flight,
Where ignorant armies clash by night.

MATTHEW ARNOLD (1822–1888)

The Moon

Beautiful Moon, with thy silvery light,
Thou seemest most charming to my sight;
As I gaze upon thee in the sky so high,
A tear of joy does moisten my eye.

Beautiful Moon, with thy silvery light,
Thou cheerest the Esquimau in the night;
For thou lettest him see to harpoon the fish,
And with them he makes a dainty dish.

Beautiful Moon, with thy silvery light,
Thou cheerest the fox in the night,
And lettest him see to steal the grey goose away
Out of the farm-yard from a stack of hay.

Beautiful Moon, with thy silvery light,
Thou cheerest the farmer in the night,
And makes his heart beat high with delight
As he views his crops by the light in the night.

Beautiful Moon, with thy silvery light,
Thou cheerest the eagle in the night,
And lettest him see to devour his prey
And carry it to his nest away.

Beautiful Moon, with thy silvery light,
Thou cheerest the mariner in the night
As he paces the deck alone,
Thinking of his dear friends at home.

Beautiful Moon, with thy silvery light,
Thou cheerest the weary traveller in the night;
For thou lightest up the wayside around
To him when he is homeward bound.

Beautiful Moon, with thy silvery light,
Thou cheerest the lovers in the night
As they walk through the shady groves alone,
Making love to each other before they go home.

Beautiful Moon, with thy silvery light,
Thou cheerest the poacher in the night;
For thou lettest him see to set his snares
To catch the rabbit and the hares.

WILLIAM MCGONAGALL (1825–1902)

A Match with the Moon

Weary already, weary miles tonight
I walked for bed: and so, to get some ease,
I dogged the flying moon with similes.
And like a wisp she doubled on my sight
In ponds; and caught in tree-tops like a kite;
And in a globe of film all liquorish
Swam full-faced like a silly silver fish; –
Last like a bubble shot the welkin's height
Where my road turned, and got behind me, and sent
My wizened shadow craning round at me
And jeered, 'So, step the measure, – one, two, three!'
And if I faced on her, looked innocent.
But just at parting, halfway down a dell,
She kissed me for goodnight. So you'll not tell.

DANTE GABRIEL ROSSETTI (1828–1882)

The Moon was But a Chin of Gold

The Moon was but a Chin of Gold
A Night or two ago –
And now she turns Her perfect Face
Upon the World below –

Her Forehead is of Amplest Blonde –
Her Cheek – a Beryl hewn –
Her Eye unto the Summer Dew
The likest I have known –

Her Lips of Amber never part –
But what must be the smile
Upon Her Friend she could confer
Were such Her Silver Will –

And what a privilege to be
But the remotest Star –
For Certainty She take Her Way
Beside Your Palace Door –

Her Bonnet is the Firmament –
The Universe – Her Shoe –
The Stars – the Trinkets at Her Belt –
Her Dimities – of Blue.

EMILY DICKINSON (1830–1886)

Lady Moon

(How to tell her age)

O Lady Moon, your horns point towards the east –
    Shine, be increased;
O Lady Moon, your horns point towards the west –
    Wane, be at rest.

CHRISTINA ROSSETTI (1830–1894)

At a Lunar Eclipse

Thy shadow, Earth, from Pole to Central Sea,
Now steals along upon the Moon's meek shine
In even monochrome and curving line
Of imperturbable serenity.

How shall I link such sun-cast symmetry
With the torn troubled form I know as thine,
That profile, placid as a brow divine,
With continents of moil and misery?

And can immense Mortality but throw
So small a shade, and Heaven's high human scheme
Be hemmed within the coasts yon arc implies?

Is such the stellar gauge of earthly show,
Nation at war with nation, brains that teem,
Heroes, and women fairer than the skies?

THOMAS HARDY (1840–1928)

To the Moon

"What have you looked at, Moon,
in your time,
Now long past your prime?"
"O, I have looked at, often looked at
Sweet, sublime,
Sore things, shudderful, night and noon
In my time."

"What have you mused on, Moon,
In your day,
So aloof, so far away?"
"O, I have mused on, often mused on
Growth, decay,
Nations alive, dead, mad aswoon,
In my day!"

"Have you much wondered, Moon,
On your rounds,
Self-wrapt, beyond Earth's bounds?"
"Yea, I have wondered, often wondered
At the sounds
Reaching me of the human tune
On my rounds."

THOMAS HARDY (1840–1928)

66

I Looked Up From My Writing

I looked up from my writing,
And gave a start to see,
As if rapt in my inditing,
The moon's full gaze on me.

Her meditative misty head
Was spectral in its air,
And I involuntarily said,
'What are you doing there?'

'Oh, I've been scanning pond and hole
And water hereabout
For the body of one with a sunken soul
Who has put his life-light out.

'Did you hear his frenzied tattle?
It was sorrow for his son
Who is slain in brutish battle,
Though he has injured none.

'And now I am curious to look
Into the blinkered mind
Of one who wants to write a book
In a world of such a kind.'

Her temper overwrought me,
And I edged to shun her view,
For I felt assured she thought me
One who should drown him too.

Thomas Hardy (1840–1928)

Moonrise

I awoke in the Midsummer not to call night,   in the white
    and the walk of the morning:
The moon, dwindled and thinned to the fringe   of a finger –
    nail held to the candle,
Or paring of paradisaical fruit,   lovely in waning but lustreless,
Stepped from the stool, drew back from the barrow,   of dark
    Maenefa the mountain;
A cusp still clasped him, a fluke yet fanged him,   entangles
    him, not quit utterly.
This was the prized, the desirable sight,   unsought, presented
    so easily,
Parted me leaf and leaf, divided me,   eyelid and eyelid of
    slumber.

GERARD MANLEY HOPKINS (1844–1889)

Clair de Lune

Your soul is a sealed garden, and there go
With masque and bergamasque fair companies
Playing on lutes and dancing and as though
Sad under their fantastic fripperies.

Though they in minor keys go carrolling
Of love the conqueror and of live boon
They seem to doubt the happiness they sing
And the song melts into the light of the moon,

The sad light of the moon, so lovely fair
That all the birds dream in the leafy shade
And the slim fountains sob into the air
Among the marble statues in the glade.

PAUL VERLAINE (1844–1896)

Translated by Arthur Symons

On Moonlit Heath and Lonesome Bank

On moonlit heath and lonesome bank
The sheep beside me graze;
And yon the gallows used to clank
Fast by the four cross ways.

A careless shepherd once would keep
The flocks by moonlight there,
And high amongst the glimmering sheep
The dead man stood on air.

They hang us now in Shrewsbury jail:
The whistles blow forlorn,
And trains all night groan on the rail
To men that die at morn.

There sleeps in Shrewsbury jail tonight,
Or wakes, as may betide,
A better lad, if things went right,
Than most that sleep outside.

And naked to the hangman's noose
The morning clocks will ring
A neck God made for other use
Than strangling in a string.

And sharp the link of life will snap,
And dead on air will stand
Heels that held up straight a chap
As treads upon the land.

So here I'll watch the night and wait
To see the morning shine,
When he will hear the stroke of eight
And not the stroke of nine;

And wish my friend as sound a sleep
As lads' I did not know,
That shepherded the moonlit sheep
A hundred years ago.

A. E. HOUSMAN (1859–1936)

White In the Moon the Long Road Lies

White in the moon the long road lies,
The moon stands blank above;
White in the moon the long road lies
That leads me from my love.

Still hangs the hedge without a gust,
Still, still the shadows stay;
My feet upon the moonlit dust
Pursue the ceaseless way.

The world is round, so travellers tell,
And straight though reach the track,
Trudge on, trudge on, 'twill all be well,
The way will guide one back.

But ere the circle homeward hies
Far, far must it remove:
White in the moon the long road lies
That leads me from my love.

A. E. HOUSMAN (1859–1936)

Clair de Lune

It comes with the force of a body blow
That the Moon is a place one cannot go.

The world is yours when you advance,
Moon, through magical August silence!

When you toss, majestic mastless wreck
In seas where black cloud-breakers break!

Ah, if my desolate soul could mount
The steps to your pure baptismal fount!

O blinded planet, fatal light
For the migratory Icarian flight!

Great sterile Eye of Suicide,
The disgusted have convened, preside;

Icy skull, make mockery
Of bald, incurable bureaucracy;

O pill of absolute lethargy,
Be dissolved in our cranial cavity!

Diana with overly Doric chlamys,
Take up thy quiver, do thy damage.

With thy one dart innoculate
Wingless Love that sleepeth late!

Planet flooded with powerful spray
May one chaste antifebrile ray

Descend and bathe my sheet tonight
So I may wash my hands of life!

JULES LAFORGUE (1860–1887)

Translated by William Jay Smith

The Cat and the Moon

The cat went here and there
And the moon spun round like a top,
And the nearest kin of the moon,
The creeping cat, looked up.
Black Minnaloushe stared at the moon,
For, wander and wail as he would,
The pure cold light in the sky
Troubled his animal blood.
Minnaloushe runs in the grass
Lifting his delicate feet.
Do you dance, Minnaloushe, do you dance?
When two close kindred meet
What better than call a dance?
Maybe the moon may learn,
Tired of that courtly fashion,
A new dance turn.
Minnaloushe creeps through the grass
From moonlit place to place,
The sacred moon overhead
Has taken a new phase.
Does Minnaloushe know that his pupils
Will pass from change to change,
And that from round to crescent,
From crescent to round they range?

Minnaloushe creeps through the grass
Alone, important and wise,
And lifts to the changing moon
His changing eyes.

W. B. YEATS (1865–1939)

At Dieppe

After Sunset

The sea lies quieted beneath
The after-sunset flush
That leaves upon the heaped grey clouds
The grape's faint purple blush.

Pale, from a little space in heaven
Of delicate ivory,
The sickle-moon and one gold star
Look down upon the sea.

ARTHUR SYMONS (1865–1945)

Mr Flood's Party

Old Eben Flood, climbing alone one night
Over the hill between the town below
And the forsaken upland hermitage
That held as much as he should ever know
On earth again of home, paused warily.
The road was his with not a native near;
And Eben, having leisure, said aloud,
For no man else in Tilbury Town to hear:

'Well, Mr Flood, we have the harvest moon
Again, and we may not have many more;
The bird is on the wing, the poet says,
And you and I have said it here before.
Drink to the bird.' He raised up to the light
The jug that he had gone so far to fill,
And answered huskily: 'Well, Mr Flood,
Since you propose it, I believe I will.'

Alone, as if enduring to the end
A valiant armor of scarred hopes outworn,
He stood there in the middle of the road
Like Roland's ghost winding a silent horn.
Below him, in the town among the trees,
Where friends of other days had honored him,

A phantom salutation of the dead
Rang thinly till old Eben's eyes were dim.

Then, as a mother lays her sleeping child
Down tenderly, fearing it may awake,
He set the jug down slowly at his feet
With trembling care, knowing that most things break;
And only when assured that on firm earth
It stood, as the uncertain lives of men
Assuredly did not, he paced away,
And with his hand extended paused again:

'Well, Mr Flood, we have not met like this
In a long time; and many a change has come
To both of us, I fear, since it last was
We had a drop together. Welcome home!'
Convivially returning with himself,
Again he raised the jug up to the light;
And with an acquiescent quaver said:
'Well, Mr Flood, if you insist, I might.'

'Only a very little, Mr Flood –
For auld lang syne. No more, sir; that will do.'
So, for the time, apparently it did,
And Eben evidently thought so too;
For soon amid the silver loneliness
Of night he lifted up his voice and sang,

Secure, with only two moons listening,
Until the whole harmonious landscape rang –

'For auld lang syne.' The weary throat gave out,
The last word wavered, and the song was done.
He raised again the jug regretfully
And shook his head, and was again alone.
There was not much that was ahead of him,
And there was nothing in the town below –
Where strangers would have shut the many doors
That many friends had opened long ago.

EDWIN ARLINGTON ROBINSON (1869–1935)

Wind and Silver

Greatly shining,
The Autumn moon floats in the thin sky;
And the fish-ponds shake their backs and flash their dragon scales
As she passes over them.

AMY LOWELL (1874–1925)

Moon-Lover

I.

The Moon is like a ping-pong ball;
I lean against the orchard wall,
And see it soar into the void,
A silky sphere of celluloid.

Then fairy fire enkindles it,
Like gossamer by taper lit,
Until it glows above the trees
As mellow as a Cheshire cheese.

And up and up I watch it press
Into appalling loneliness;
Like realms of ice without a stain,
A corpse moon comes to life again.

Ruthless it drowns a sturdy star
That seeks its regal way to bar;
Seeming with conscious power to grow,
And sweeter, purer, gladder glow.

Dreaming serenely up the sky
Until exultantly on high,
It shimmers with superb delight,
The silver navel of the night.

II.

I have a compact to commune
A monthly midnight with the Moon;
Into its face I stare and stare,
And find sweet understanding there.

As quiet as a toad I sit
And tell my tale of days to it;
The tessellated yarn I've spun
In thirty spells of star and sun.

And the Moon listens pensively,
As placid as a lamb to me;
Until I think there's just us two
In silver world of mist and dew.

In all of spangled space but I
To stare moon-struck into the sky;
Of billion beings I alone
To praise the Moon as still as stone.

And seal a bond between us two,
Closer than mortal ever knew;
For as mute masses I intone
The Moon is mine and mine alone.

III.

To know the Moon as few men may,
One must be just a little *fey*;
And for our friendship's sake I'm glad
That I am just a trifle mad.

And one with all the wild, wise things,
The furtive folk of fur and wings,
That hold the Moon within their eyes,
And make it nightly sacrifice.

O I will watch the maiden Moon
Dance on the sea with silver shoon;
But with the Queen Moon I will keep
My tryst when all the world's asleep.

As I have kept by land and sea
That tryst for half a century;
Entranced in sibylline suspense
Beyond a world of common sense.

Until one night the Moon alone
Will look upon a graven stone . . .
I wonder will it miss me then,
Its lover more than other men?

Or will my wistful ghost be there,
Down ages dim to stare and stare,
On silver nights without a stir –
The Moon's Eternal Worshipper?

ROBERT SERVICE (1874–1958)

Moon Compasses

I stole forth dimly in the dripping pause
Between two downpours to see what there was.
And a masked moon had spread down compass rays
To a cone mountain in the midnight haze,
As if the final estimate were hers;
And as it measured in her calipers,
The mountain stood exalted in its place.
So love will take between the hands a face . . .

ROBERT FROST (1874–1963)

Liberty

The last light has gone out of the world, except
This moonlight lying on the grass like frost
Beyond the brink of the tall elm's shadow.
It is as if everything else had slept
Many an age, unforgotten and lost –
The men that were, the things done, long ago,
All I have thought; and but the moon and I
Live yet and here stand idle over a grave
Where all is buried. Both have liberty
To dream what we could do if we were free
To do some thing we had desired long,
The moon and I. There's none less free than who
Does nothing and has nothing else to do,
Being free only for what is not to his mind,
And nothing is to his mind. If every hour
Like this one passing that I have spent among
The wiser others when I have forgot
To wonder whether I was free or not,
Were piled before me, and not lost behind,
And I could take and carry them away
I should be rich; or if I had the power
To wipe out every one and not again
Regret, I should be rich to be so poor.
And yet I still am half in love with pain,

With what is imperfect, with both tears and mirth,
With things that have an end, with life and earth,
And this moon that leaves me dark within the door.

EDWARD THOMAS (1878–1917)

Overheard On A Saltmarsh

Nymph, nymph, what are your beads?

Green glass, goblin.   Why do you stare at them?

Give them me.

                    No.

Give them me.   Give them me.

                                    No.

Then I will howl all night in the reeds,
Lie in the mud and howl for them.

Goblin, why do you love them so?

They are better than stars or water,
Better than voices of winds that sing,
Better than any man's fair daughter,
Your green glass beads on a silver ring.

Hush, I stole them out of the moon.

Give me your beads, I want them.

                                No.

I will howl in a deep lagoon
For your green glass beads, I love them so.
Give them me.   Give them.

                                No.

HAROLD MONRO (1879–1932)

It was the Lovely Moon

It was the lovely moon – she lifted
Slowly her white brow among
Bronze cloud-waves that ebbed and drifted
Faintly, faintlier afar.
Calm she looked, yet pale with wonder,
Sweet in unwonted thoughtfulness,
Watching the earth that dwindled under
Faintly, faintlier afar.
It was the lovely moon that lovelike
Hovered over the wandering, tired
Earth, her bosom grey and dovelike,
Hovering beautiful as a dove . . .
The lovely moon: her soft light falling
Lightly on roof and poplar and pine –
Tree to tree whispering and calling,
Wonderful in the silvery shine
Of the round, lovely, thoughtful moon.

JOHN FREEMAN (1880–1929)

Autumn

A touch of cold in the autumn night –
I walked abroad,
And saw the ruddy moon lean over a hedge
Like a red-faced farmer.
I did not stop to speak, but nodded,
And round about were the wistful stars
With white faces like town children.

T. E. HULME (1883–1917)

Morning Song

A diamond of a morning
Waked me an hour too soon;
Dawn had taken in the stars
And left the faint white moon.

O white moon, you are lonely,
It is the same with me,
But we have the world to roam over,
Only the lonely are free.

SARA TEASDALE (1884–1933)

Moon's Ending

Moon, worn thin to the width of a quill,
In the dawn clouds flying,
How good to go, light into light, and still
Giving light, dying.

SARA TEASDALE (1884–1933)

Phases of the Moon

Once upon a time I heard
That the flying moon was a Phoenix bird;
Thus she sails through windy skies,
Thus in the willow's arms she lies;
Turn to the East or turn to the West
In many trees she makes her nest.
When she's but a pearly thread
Look among birch leaves overhead;
When she dies in yellow smoke
Look in a thunder-smitten oak;
But in May when the moon is full
Bright as water and white as wool,
Look for her where she loves to be
Asleep in a high magnolia tree.

ELINOR WYLIE (1885–1928)

Week-Night Service

The five old bells
Are hurrying and eagerly calling,
Imploring, protesting
They know, but clamorously falling
Into gabbling incoherence, never resting,
Like spattering showers from a bursten sky-rocket dropping
In splashes of sound, endlessly, never stopping.

The silver moon
That somebody has spun so high
To settle the question, yes or no, has caught
In the net of the night's balloon,
And sits with a smooth bland smile up there in the sky
Smiling at naught,
Unless the winking star that keeps her company
Makes little jests at the bells' insanity,
As if he knew aught!

The patient Night
Sits indifferent, hugged in her rags,
She neither knows nor cares
Why the old church sobs and brags;
The light distresses her eyes, and tears
Her old blue cloak, as she crouches and covers her face,
Smiling, perhaps, if we knew it, at the bells' loud clattering disgrace.

The wise old trees
Drop their leaves with a faint, sharp hiss of contempt,
While a car at the end of the street goes by with a laugh;
As by degrees
The poor bells cease, and the Night is exempt,
And the stars can chaff
The ironic moon at their ease, while the dim old church
Is peopled with shadows and sounds and ghosts that lurch
In its cenotaph.

D. H. LAWRENCE (1885–1930)

Red Moon-Rise

The train, in running across the weald, has fallen into a steadier stroke,
So even, it beats like silence, and sky and earth in one unbroke
Embrace of darkness lie around, and crushed between them, all the loose
And littered lettering of trees and hills and houses closed, and we can use
The open book of landscape no more, for the covers of darkness have shut upon
Its figured pages, and sky and earth and all between are closed in one.

And we are crushed between the covers, we close our eyes and say "Hush!" We try
To escape in sleep the terror of this great bivalve darkness, and we lie
Rounded like pearls, for sleep. – And then, from between shut lips of darkness, red
As if from the womb the slow moon rises, as if the twin-walled darkness had bled
In a new night-spasm of birth, and given us this new red moon-rise
Which lies on the knees of the night-time ruddy, and makes us hide our eyes.

The train beats frantic in haste, and struggles away
From this rosy terror of birth that has slid down
From out of the loins of night, to glow in our way
Like a portent; but, Lord, I am glad, so glad, I drown
My fear in accepting the portent. The train can now
Not pass the red moon risen, and I am glad,
Glad as the Magi were when they saw the brow
Of the hot-born infant bless the folly which had
Led them thither to peace;

                                        for now I know
The world within worlds is a womb, whence issues all
The shapeliness that decks us here-below:
And the same fire that boils within this ball
Of earth, and quickens all herself with flowers,
Is womb-fire in the stiffened clay of us:

And every flash of thought that we and ours
Send suddenly out, and every gesture, does
Fly like a spark into the womb of passion,
To start a birth, from joy of the begetting.

World within worlds a womb, that gives and takes;
Gives us all forth, that we may give again
The seed of life incarnate, that falls and wakes
Within the womb, new shapes, and then, new men.

And pangs of birth, and joy of the begetting,
And sweat of labour, and the meanest fashion
Of fretting or of gladness, shows the jetting
Of a trail of our small fire on the darkened sky
Where we can see it, our fire to the innermost fire
Leaping like spray, in the return of passion.

And even in the watery shells that lie
Alive within the oozy under-mire,
A grain of this same fire we can descry
Spurting to soothe the womb's unslaked desire.

And so, from out the screaming birds that fly
Across the heavens when the storm leaps higher,
And from the swirling, angry folk that try
To come at last to that which they require,

And from men that dance, and the girls that laugh,
And the flower that puts its tongue out, and fern that puffs
Dust as the puff-ball does, and birds that chaff
And chitter, and wind that shakes and cuffs
The branches, invisible seed of experience blows
Into the womb of the worlds, that nothing knows.

And though it be love's wet blue eyes that cry
To the other love, to relinquish his desire,
Even there I see, a blue spark that will fly
Into the womb, to kindle an unknown fire.

D. H. LAWRENCE (1885–1930)

Moonrise

And who has seen the moon, who has not seen
Her rise from out the chamber of the deep,
Flushed and grand and naked, as from the chamber
Of finished bridegroom, seen her rise and throw
Confession of delight upon the wave,
Littering the waves with her own superscription
Of bliss, till all her lambent beauty shakes towards us
Spread out and known at last, and we are sure
That beauty is a thing beyond the grave,
That perfect, bright experience never falls
To nothingness, and time will dim the moon
Sooner than our full consummation here
In this odd life will tarnish or pass away.

D. H. LAWRENCE (1885–1930)

A Poplar and the Moon

There stood a Poplar, tall and straight;
The fair, round Moon, uprisen late,
Made the long shadow on the grass
A ghostly bridge 'twixt heaven and me.
But May, with slumbrous nights, must pass;
And blustering winds will strip the tree.
And I've no magic to express
The moment of that loveliness;
So from these words you'll never guess
The stars and lilies I could see.

SIEGFRIED SASSOON (1886–1967)

Sleeping Out: Full Moon

They sleep . . .
I cower to the earth, I waking, I only.
High and cold thou dreamest, O queen, high-dreaming and lonely.

We have slept too long, who can hardly win
The white one flame, and the night-long crying;
The viewless passers; the world's low sighing
With desire, with yearning,
To the fire unburning,
To the heatless fire, to the flameless ecstasy . . .

Helpless I lie.
And around me the feet of thy watchers tread.
There is a rumour and a radiance of wings above my head,
An intolerable radiance of wings above my head,
An intolerable radiance of wings . . .

All the earth grows fire,
White lips of desire
Brushing cool on the forehead, croon slumbrous things.
Earth fades; and the air is thrilled with ways,
Dewy paths full of comfort. And radiant bands,
The gracious presence of friendly hands,
Help the blind one, the glad one, who stumbles and strays,

Stretching wavering hands up, up, through the praise
Of a myriad silver trumpets, through cries,
To all glory, to all gladness, to the infinite height,
To the gracious, the unmoving, the mother eyes,
And the laughter, and the lips of light.

RUPERT BROOKE (1887–1915)

Clouds

Down the blue night the unending columns press
In noiseless tumult, break and wave and flow,
Now tread the far South, or lift rounds
Up to the white moon's hidden loveliness.

Some pause in their grave wandering comradeless,
And turn with profound gesture vague and slow,
As who would pray good for the world, but know
Their benedictions empty as they bless.

They say that the Dead die not, but remain
Near to the rich heirs of their grief and mirth.
I think they ride the calm mid-heaven, as these,
In wise majestic melancholy train,
And watch the moon, and the still-raging seas,
And men, coming and going on the earth.

RUPERT BROOKE (1887–1915)

Hooded Night

At night, toward dawn, all the lights of the shore have died,
And a wind moves. Moves in the dark
The sleeping power of the ocean, no more beastlike than manlike,
Not to be compared; itself and itself.
Its breath blown shoreward huddles the world with a fog; no stars
Dance in heaven; no ship's light glances.
I see the heavy granite bodies of the rocks of the headland,
That were ancient before Egypt had pyramids,
Bulk on the grey of the sky, and beyond them the jets of young trees
I planted the year of the Versailles peace.
But here is the final unridiculous peace. Before the first man
Here were the stones, the ocean, the cypresses,
And the pallid region in the stone-rough dome of fog where the moon
Falls on the west. Here is reality.
The other is a spectral episode: after the inquisitive animal's
Amusements are quiet: the dark glory.

ROBINSON JEFFERS (1887–1962)

The New Moon

What have you got in your knapsack fair,
White moon, bright moon, pearling the air,
Spinning your bobbins and fabrics free,
Fleet moon, sweet moon, in the sea?
Turquoise and beryl and rings of gold,
Clear moon, dear moon, ne'er to be sold?
Roses and lilies, romance and love,
Still moon, chill moon, swinging above?
Slender your feet as a white bird's throat,
High moon, shy moon, drifting your boat
Into the murk of the world awhile,
Slim moon, dim moon, adding a smile.
Tender your eyes as a maiden's kiss,
Fine moon, wine moon, no one knows this,
Under the spell of your witchery,
Dream moon, cream moon, first he kissed me.

ZORA CROSS (1890–1964)

If Still Your Orchards Bear

Brother, that breathe the August air
Ten thousand years from now,
And smell – if still your orchards bear
Tart apples on the bough –

The early windfall under the tree,
And see the red fruit shine,
I cannot think your thoughts will be
Much different from mine –

Should at that moment the full moon
Step forth upon the hill,
And memories hard to bear at noon,
By moonlight harder still,

Form in the shadow of the trees –
Things that you could not spare
And live, or so you thought, yet these
All gone, and you still there,

A man no longer what he was,
Nor yet the thing he'd planned,
The chilly apple from the grass
Warmed by your living hand –

I think you will have need of tears;
I think they will not flow;
Supposing in ten thousand years
Men ache, as they do now.

EDNA ST VINCENT MILLAY (1892–1950)

Full Moon

She is wearing coral taffeta trousers
Someone has bought her from Isfahan.
And the little gold coat with pomegranate blossoms,
And the coral-hafted feather fan,
But she ran down a Kentish lane in the moonlight,
And skipped in the pool of moon as she ran.

She cared not a rap for all the big planets,
For Betelgeuse or Aldebaran,
And all the big planets cared nothing for her,
That small impertinent charlatan,
As she climbed on a Kentish stile in the moonlight,
And laughed at the sky through the sticks of her fan.

VITA SACKVILLE-WEST (1892–1962)

Ars Poetica

A poem should be palpable and mute
As a globed fruit,

Dumb
As old medallions to the thumb,

Silent as the sleeve-worn stone
Of casement ledges where the moss has grown —

A poem should be wordless
As the flight of birds.

*

A poem should be motionless in time
As the moon climbs,

Leaving, as the moon releases
Twig by twig the night-entangled trees,

Leaving, as the moon behind the winter leaves,
Memory by memory the mind —

A poem should be motionless in time
As the moon climbs.

*

A poem should be equal to:
Not true.

For all the history of grief
An empty doorway and a maple leaf.

For love
The leaning grasses and two lights above the sea –

A poem should not mean –
But be.

ARCHIBALD MACLEISH (1892–1982)

Voyage to the Moon

Presence among us,

      Wanderer in our skies,

dazzle of silver in our leaves and on our
waters silver,

      O

silver evasion in our farthest thought –
"the visiting moon" . . . "the glimpses of the moon" . . .

and we have touched you!

      From the first of time,
before the first of time, before the
first men tasted time, we thought of you,
you were a wonder to us, unattainable,
a longing past the reach of longing,
a light beyond our light, our lives – perhaps
a meaning to us . . .

      Now
our hands have touched you in your depth of night.

Three days and nights we journeyed,
steered by farthest stars, climbed outward,
crossed the invisible tide-rip where the floating dust
falls one way or the other in the void between,

followed that other down, encountered
cold, faced death- unfathomable emptiness . . .

Then, the fourth day evening, we descended,
made fast, set foot at dawn upon your beaches,
sifted between our fingers your cold sand.

We stand here in the dusk, the cold, the silence . . .

and here, as at the first of time, we lift our heads.
Over us, more beautiful than the moon, a
moon, a wonder to us, unattainable,
a longing past the reach of longing,
a light beyond our light, our lives – perhaps
a meaning to us . . .

      O a meaning!
over us on those silent beaches the bright
earth,

      presence among us.

ARCHIBALD MACLEISH (1892–1982)

who knows if the moon's . . .

who knows if the moon's
a balloon, coming out of a keen city
in the sky – filled with pretty people?
(and if you and i should

get into it, if they
should take me and take you into their balloon,
why then
we'd go up higher with all the pretty people

than houses and steeples and clouds:
go sailing
away and away sailing into a keen
city which nobody's ever visited, where

always
it's
Spring) and everyone's
in love and flowers pick themselves

E. E. CUMMINGS (1894–1962)

Full Moon

As I walked out that sultry night,
I heard the stroke of One.
The moon, attained to her full height,
Stood beaming like the sun:
She exorcized the ghostly wheat
To mute assent in love's defeat,
Whose tryst had now begun.

The fields lay sick beneath my tread,
A tedious owlet cried,
A nightingale above my head
With this or that replied –
Like man and wife who nightly keep
Inconsequent debate in sleep
As they dream side by side.

Your phantom wore the moon's cold mask,
My phantom wore the same;
Forgetful of the feverish task
In hope of which they came,
Each image held the other's eyes
And watched a grey distraction rise
To cloud the eager flame.

To cloud the eager flame of love,
To fog the shining gate;
They held the tyrannous queen above
Sole mover of their fate,
They glared as marble statues glare
Across the tessellated air
Or down the halls of state.

And now warm earth was Arctic sea,
Each breath came dagger-keen;
Two bergs of glinting ice were we,
The broad moon sailed between;
There swam the mermaids, tailed and finned,
And love went by upon the wind
As though it had not been.

ROBERT GRAVES (1895–1985)

The Cruel Moon

The cruel Moon hangs out of reach
Up above the shadowy beech.
Her face is stupid, but her eye
Is small and sharp and very sly.
Nurse says the Moon can drive you mad?
No, that's a silly story, lad!
Though she be angry, though she would
Destroy all England if she could,
Yet think, what damage can she do
Hanging there so far from you?
Don't heed what frightened nurses say:
Moons hang much too far away.

ROBERT GRAVES (1895–1985)

An Old Woman Speaks of the Moon

She was urgent to speak of the moon: she offered delight
And wondering praise to be shared by the girl in the shop,
Lauding the goddess who blessed her each sleepless night
Greater and brighter till full: but the girl could not stop.

She turned and looked up in my face, and hastened to cry
How beautiful was the orb, how the constant glow
Comforted in the cold night the old waking eye:
How fortunate she, whose lodging was placed that so

She in the lonely night, in her lonely age,
She from her poor lean bed might behold the undying
Letter of loveliness written on heaven's page,
The sharp silver arrows leap down to where she was lying.

The dying spoke love to the immortal, the foul to the fair,
The withered to the still-flowering, the bound to the free:
The nipped worm to the silver swan that sails through the air:
And I took it as good, and a happy omen to me.

RUTH PITTER (1897–1922)

120

The Moon Sails Out

When the moon sails out
the church bells die away
and the paths overgrown
with brush appear.

When the moon sails out
the waters cover the earth
and the heart feels it is
a little island in the infinite.

No one eats oranges
under the full moon.
The right things are fruits
green and chilled.

When the moon sails out
with a hundred faces all the same,
the coins made of silver
break out in sobs in the pocket.

FEDERICO GARCÍA LORCA (1898–1936)

Translated by Robert Bly

Chaplinesque

We will make our meek adjustments,
Contented with such random consolations
As the wind deposits
In slithered and too ample pockets.

For we can still love the world, who find
A famished kitten on the step, and know
Recesses for it from the fury of the street,
Or warm torn elbow coverts.

We will sidestep, and to the final smirk
Dally the doom of that inevitable thumb
That slowly chafes its puckered index toward us,
Facing the dull squint with what innocence
And what surprise!

And yet these fine collapses are not lies
More than the pirouettes of any pliant cane;
Our obsequies are, in a way, no enterprise.
We can evade you, and all else but the heart:
What blame to us if the heart live on.

The game enforces smirks; but we have seen
The moon in lonely alleys make
A grail of laughter of an empty ash can,
And through all sound of gaiety and quest
Have heard a kitten in the wilderness.

HART CRANE (1899–1932)

Meditation

I have drawn my hands away
Toward peace and the grey margins of the day.
The andante of vain hopes and lost regret
Falls like slow rain that whispers to forget –
Like a song that neither questions nor replies
It laves with coolness tarnished lips and eyes.

I have drawn my hands away
At last to touch the ungathered rose. O stay,
Moment of dissolving happiness! Astir
Already in the sky, night's chorister
Has brushed a petal from the jasmine moon,
And the heron has passed by, alas, how soon!

I have drawn my hands away
Like ships for guidance in the lift and spray
Of stars that urge them toward an unknown goal.
Drift, O wakeful one, O restless soul,
Until the glittering white open hand
Of heaven thou shalt read and understand.

HART CRANE (1899–1932)

Nightwalker

Pick my steps, Moon,
And shoe me. Heavy water my heart makes
That would sail true
To everything at once, for no sake but for all sakes.

So much noise and water
Sailing dog-lipped the capes of whales in white
Scud; shoe me, Moon,
And show bright the strands beyond where you fall quietly.

PADRAIC FALLON (1905–1974)

Make This Night . . .

Make this night loveable,
Moon, and with eye single
Looking down from up there
Bless me. One especial,
And friends everywhere.

With a cloudless brightness
Surround our absences;
Innocent be our sleeps,
Watched by great still spaces,
White hills, glittering deeps.

Parted by circumstance,
Grant each your indulgence
That we may meet in dreams
For talk, for dalliance,
By warm hearths, by cool streams.

Shine lest tonight any,
In the dark suddenly,
Wake alone in a bed
To hear his own fury
Wishing his love were dead.

W. H. AUDEN (1907–1973)

Moon Landing

It's natural the Boys should whoop it up for
so huge a phallic triumph, an adventure
it would not have occurred to women
to think worth while, made possible only

because we like huddling in gangs and knowing
the exact time: yes, our sex may in fairness
hurrah the deed, although the motives
that primed it were somewhat less than menschlich.

A grand gesture. But what does it period?
What does it osse? We were always adroiter
with objects than lives, and more facile
at courage than kindness: from the moment

the first flint was flaked this landing was merely
a matter of time. But our selves, like Adam's,
still don't fit us exactly, modern
only in this – our lack of decorum.

Homer's heroes were certainly no braver
than our Trio, but more fortunate: Hector
was excused the insult of having
his valour covered by television.

Worth going to see? I can well believe it.
Worth seeing? Mneh! I once rode through a desert
and was not charmed: give me a watered
lively garden, remote from blatherers

about the New, the von Brauns and their ilk, where
on August mornings I can count the morning
glories where to die has a meaning,
and no engine can shift my perspective.

Unsmudged, thank God, my Moon still queens the Heavens
as She ebbs and fulls, a Presence to glop at,
Her Old Man, made of grit not protein,
still visits my Austrian several

with His old detachment, and the old warnings
still have power to scare me: Hybris comes to
an ugly finish, Irreverence
is a greater oaf than Superstition.

Our apparatniks will continue making
the usual squalid mess called History:
all we can pray for is that artists,
chefs and saints may still appear blithe to it.

W. H. AUDEN (1907–1973)

Insomnia

The moon in the bureau mirror
looks out a million miles
(and perhaps with pride, at herself,
but she never, never smiles)
far and away beyond sleep, or
perhaps she's a daytimer sleeper.

By the universe deserted,
she'd tell it to go to hell,
and she'd find a body of water,
or a mirror, on which to dwell.
So wrap up care in a cobweb
and drop it down the well

into that world inverted
where left is always right,
where the shadows are really the body,
where we stay awake all night,
where the heavens are shallow as the sea
is now deep, and you love me.

ELIZABETH BISHOP (1911–1979)

A Nameless Woman

I wish to be a nameless woman
way out on a small hillside.
With gourd-vines on the roof of my cottage,
pumpkins and cucumbers in a hemp-garden,
the moon invited into my yard
over a fence made of roses,
and my arms full of stars;
the owl-hooting dark will not make me lonely.

In a village where the train never stops,
eating millet-cake soaked in a brass basin,
talking with a close friend until late at night
about the secrets of the fox-haunted mountains,
while a shaggy dog barks at the moon,
I shall be happier than a queen.

NO CH'ONMYONG (1912–1957)

Translated by Ko Won

The Moon In Lleyn

The last quarter of the moon
of Jesus gave way
to the dark; the serpent
digests the egg. Here
on my knees in this stone
church, that is full only
of the silent congregation
of shadows and the sea's
sound, it is easy to believe
Yeats was right. Just as though
choirs had not sung, shells
have swallowed them; the tide laps
at the Bible; the bell fetches
no people to the brittle miracle
of the bread. The sand is waiting
for the running back of the grains
in the wall into its blond
glass. Religion is over, and
what will emerge from the body
of the new moon, no one
can say.
         But a voice sounds
in my ear: Why so fast,
mortal? These very seas

are baptised. The parish
has a saint's name time cannot
unfrock. In cities that
have outgrown their promise people
are becoming pilgrims
again, if not to this place,
then to the recreation of it
in their own spirits. You must remain
kneeling. Even as this moon
making its way through the earth's
cumbersome shadow, prayer, too,
has its phases.

R. S. THOMAS (1913–2000)

Landing on the Moon

When in the mask of night there shone that cut,
we were riddled. A probe reached down
and stroked some nerve in us,
as if the glint from a wizard's eye, of silver,
slanted out of the mask of the unknown –
pit of riddles, the scratch-marked sky.

When, albino bowl on cloth of jet,
it spilled its virile rays,
our eyes enlarged, our blood reared with the waves.
We craved its secret, but unreachable
it held away from us, chilly and frail.
Distance kept it magnate. Enigma made it white.

When we learned to read it with our rod,
reflected light revealed
a lead mirror, a bruised shield
seamed with scars and shadow-soiled.
A half faced sycophant, its glitter borrowed
rode around our throne.

On the moon there shines earth light
as moonlight shines upon the earth . . .
If on its obsidian we set our weightless foot,

and sniff no wind, and lick no rain
and feel no gauze between us and the Fire
will we trot its grassless skull, sick for the homelike shade?

Naked to the earth-beam we shall be,
who have arrived to map an apparition,
who walk upon the forehead of a myth.
Can flesh rub with symbol? If our ball
be iron, and not light, our earliest wish
eclipses. Dare we land upon a dream?

MAY SWENSON (1913–1989)

Clown In The Moon

My tears are like the quiet drift
Of petals from some magic rose;
And all my grief flows from the rift
Of unremembered skies and snows.

I think, that if I touched the earth,
It would crumble;
It is so sad and beautiful,
So tremulously like a dream.

DYLAN THOMAS (1914–1953)

In My Craft or Sullen Art

In my craft or sullen art
Exercised in the still night
When only the moon rages
And the lovers lie abed
With all their griefs in their arms,
I labour by singing light
Not for ambition or bread
Or the strut and trade of charms
On the ivory stages
But for the common wages
Of their most secret heart.

Not for the proud man apart
From the raging moon I write
On these spindrift pages
Nor for the towering dead
With their nightingales and psalms
But for the lovers, their arms
Round the griefs of the ages
Who pay no praise or wages
Nor heed my craft or art.

DYLAN THOMAS (1914–1953)

The Moon and the Night and the Men

On the night of the Belgian surrender the moon rose
Late, a delayed moon, and a violent moon
For the English or the American beholder;
The French beholder. It was a cold night,
People put on their wraps, the troops were cold
No doubt, despite the calendar, no doubt
Numbers of refugees coughed, and the sight
Or sound of some killed others. A cold night.

On Outer Drive there was an accident:
A stupid well-intentioned man turned sharp
Right and abruptly he became an angel
Fingering an unfamiliar harp,
Or screamed in hell, or was nothing at all.
Do not imagine this is unimportant.
He was a part of the night, part of the land,
Part of the bitter and exhausted ground
Out of which memory grows.

                      Michael and I
Stared at each other over chess, and spoke
As little as possible, and drank and played.
The chessmen caught in the European eye,
Neither of us I think had a free look

Although the game was fair. The move one made
It was difficult at last to keep one's mind on.
'. . . hurt and unhappy' said the man in London.
We said to each other, The time is coming near
When none shall have books or music, none his dear,
And only a fool will speak aloud his mind.
History is approaching a speechless end,
As Henry Adams said. Adams was right.

All this occurred on the night when Leopold
Fulfilled the treachery four years before
Begun – or was he well-intentioned, more
Roadmaker to hell than king? At any rate,
The moon came up late and the night was cold,
Many men died – although we know the fate
Of none, nor of anyone, and the war
Goes on, and the moon in the breast of man is cold.

JOHN BERRYMAN (1914–1972)

Translunar Space March

The interior of Pioneer-10,
as it courses smoothly beyond the Moon
at 31,000 miles an hour,
is calm and full of instruments.
No crew for the two-year trip to Jupiter,
but in the middle of the picture
a gold plaque, six inches by nine,
remedies the omission. Against a diagram
of the planets and pulsars of our solar system and galaxy,
and superimposed on an outline of the spacecraft
in which they are not travelling
(and would not be as they are shown
even if they were) two quaint nude figures
face the camera. A deodorized American man
with apologetic genitals and no pubic hair
holds up a banana-like right hand
in Indian greeting, at his side a woman,
smaller, and also with no pubic hair,
is not allowed to hold up her hand,
stands with one leg off-centre, and
is obviously an inferior sort
of the same species. However,
the male chauvinist pig
has a sullen expression, and the woman

is faintly smiling, so
interplanetary intelligences may still have homework.
Meanwhile, on to the Red Spot,
Pluto, and eternity.

EDWIN MORGAN (1920–)

Sad Steps

Groping back to bed after a piss
I part thick curtains, and am startled by
The rapid clouds, the moon's cleanliness.

Four o'clock: wedge-shadowed gardens lie
Under a cavernous, a wind-picked sky.
There's something laughable about this,

The way the moon dashes through clouds that blow
Loosely as cannon-smoke to stand apart
(Stone-coloured light sharpening the roofs below)

High and preposterous and separate –
Lozenge of love! Medallion of art!
O wolves of memory! Immensements! No,

One shivers slightly, looking up there.
The hardness and the brightness and the plain
Far-reaching singleness of that wide stare

Is a reminder of the strength and pain
Of being young; that it can't come again,
But is for others undiminished somewhere.

PHILIP LARKIN (1922–1985)

Moon Object

After the astronaut's intrusion of moonlight, after
the metal flag, the computer-speeches – this little booty.

Is it really from the moon? Identify it if you can.
Test it, blue-eyed scientist, between finger and thumb.

Through a rainy city a car continues numb.
Its radio blanks out beneath a bridge.

In a restaurant, your colleague with a cold
is trying to taste his own saliva.

On the school piano, your wife's index finger
sinks the highest note. She hears the sound of felt.

Blue eyes, let your own finger and your thumb
slip and slide about it devilishly.

Don't you feel the gravity of the moon?
Say a prayer for the dead and murmur a vow.

Change your white coat for a purple cloak
and cage yourself a peacock or a gnat.

No, rational, you sniff it. But some holes in your front-brain
have been scooped out. A moon-howling dog would know.

Blue eyes, observe it again. See its dull appearance
and be careful: it could be cursed, it could be sleeping.

Awake, it might change colour like a lampshade
turned on, seething – suddenly moon-plugged.

Scientist, something rum has happened to you.
Your right eyes and left eyes have been switched around.

Back home, if you dialled your own number now,
a shameless voice would reply, 'Who? Who?'

DANNIE ABSE (1923–)

The Well

At sixteen I believed the moonlight
could change me if it would.
     I moved my head
on the pillow, even moved my bed
as the moon slowly
crossed the open lattice.

I wanted beauty, a dangerous
gleam of steel, my body thinner,
my pale face paler.
     I moonbathed
diligently, as others sunbathe.
But the moon's unsmiling stare
kept me awake. Mornings,
I was flushed and cross.

It was on dark nights of deep sleep
that I dreamed the most, sunk in the well,
and woke rested, and if not beautiful,
filled with some other power.

DENISE LEVERTOV (1923–1997)

In Praise of Creation

That one bird, one star,
The one flash of the tiger's eye
Purely assert what they are,
Without ceremony testify.

Testify to order, to rule –
How the birds mate at one time only,
How the sky is, for a certain time, full
Of birds, the moon sometimes cut thinly.

And the tiger trapped in the cage of his skin,
Watchful over creation, rests
For the blood to pound, the drums to begin,
Till the tiger's shadow casts

A darkness over him, a passion, a scent,
The world goes turning, turning, the season
Sieves earth to its one sure element
And the blood beats beyond reason.

Then quiet, and birds folding their wings,
The new moon waiting for years to be stared at here,
The season sinks to satisfied things –
Man with his mind ajar.

ELIZABETH JENNINGS (1926–2001)

You Can Have It

My brother comes home from work
and climbs the stairs to our room.
I can hear the bed groan and his shoes drop
one by one. You can have it, he says.

The moonlight streams in the window
and his unshaven face is whitened
like the face of the moon. He will sleep
long after noon and waken to find me gone.

Thirty years will pass before I remember
that moment when suddenly I knew each man
has one brother who dies when he sleeps
and sleeps when he rises to face this life,

and that together they are only one man
sharing a heart that always labors, hands
yellowed and cracked, a mouth that gasps
for breath and asks, Am I gonna make it?

All night at the ice plant he had fed
the chute its silvery blocks, and then I
stacked cases of orange soda for the children
of Kentucky, one gray boxcar at a time

with always two more waiting. We were twenty
for such a short time and always in
the wrong clothes, crusted with dirt
and sweat. I think now we were never twenty.

In 1948 in the city of Detroit, founded
by de la Mothe Cadillac for the distant purposes
of Henry Ford, no one wakened or died,
no one walked the streets or stoked a furnace,

for there was no such year, and now
that year has fallen off all the old newspapers,
calendars, doctors' appointments, bonds,
wedding certificates, drivers licenses.

The city slept. The snow turned to ice.
The ice to standing pools or rivers
racing in the gutters. Then bright grass rose
between the thousands of cracked squares,

and that grass died. I give you back 1948.
I give you all the years from then
to the coming one. Give me back the moon
with its frail light falling across a face.

Give me back my young brother, hard
and furious, with wide shoulders and a curse
for God and burning eyes that look upon
all creation and say, You can have it.

PHILIP LEVINE (1928–)

Full Moon and Little Frieda

A cool small evening shrunk to a dog bark and the clank of a bucket –

And you listening,
A spider's web, tense for the dew's touch.
A pail lifted, still and brimming – mirror
To tempt a first star to a tremor.

Cows are going home in the lane there, looping the hedges with their
    warm wreaths of breath –
A dark river of blood, many boulders,
Balancing unspilled milk.

'Moon!' you cry suddenly, 'Moon! Moon!'

The moon has stepped back like an artist gazing amazed at a work

That points at him amazed.

TED HUGHES (1930–1998)

The Harvest Moon

The flame-red moon, the harvest moon,
Rolls along the hills, gently bouncing,
A vast balloon,
Till it takes off, and sinks upward
To lie in the bottom of the sky, like a gold doubloon.

The harvest moon has come,
Booming softly through heaven, like a bassoon.
And earth replies all night, like a deep drum.

So people can't sleep,
So they go out where elms and oak trees keep
A kneeling vigil, in a religious hush.
The harvest moon has come.

And all the moonlit cows and all the sheep
Stare up at her petrified, while she swells
Filling heaven, as if red hot, and sailing
Closer and closer like the end of the world

Till the gold fields of stiff wheat
Cry 'We are ripe, reap us!' and the rivers
Sweat from the melting hills.

TED HUGHES (1930–1998)

August Full Moon

Whichever I choose to look out from, here in my study,
Where the desk is placed in a corner between two windows,
I see her, the August full moon. Labouring towards
This completion, since yesterday she has freed herself,
Purged and dissolved the humours distorting her shape,
Making her swollen and clumsy, darkened from yellow
Of faded leather into the streaked, mottled red of
An old woman's cheek. As if she had discharged her poisons
Into my veins, today I was almost demented,
Sodden, confused, barely awake or able to move
About the house and garden. But the moon, silver
In a starless sky, windless night after a day
Of stasis and sunshine, is disdainful of such effects
On whoever is weak enough to suffer this draining
Connexion to her necessities: I, who sit yawning
And trembling in spite of the heat of a perfect evening,
Who will soon go, defeated, to bed, to escape
Beyond dreams into emptiness from this moment
When the whole universe combines in haughty balance
And self-sufficiency to reject me, to wait
Until all the spheres lurch forward one notch and leave space
Again for an opening that hope and change might stream through.

RUTH FAINLIGHT (1931–)

The Moon and the Yew Tree

This is the light of the mind, cold and planetary.
The trees of the mind are black. The light is blue.
The grasses unload their griefs on my feet as if I were God
Pricking my ankles and murmuring of their humility.
Fumy, spiritous mists inhabit this place.
Separated from my house by a row of headstones.
I simply cannot see where there is to get to.

The moon is no door. It is a face in its own right,
White as a knuckle and terribly upset.
It drags the sea after it like a dark crime; it is quiet
With the O-gape of complete despair. I live here.
Twice on Sunday, the bells startle the sky –
Eight great tongues affirming the resurrection
At the end, they soberly bong out their names.

The yew tree points up, it has a Gothic shape.
The eyes lift after it and find the moon.
The moon is my mother. She is not sweet like Mary.
Her blue garments unloose small bats and owls.
How I would like to believe in tenderness –
The face of the effigy, gentled by candles,
Bending, on me in particular, its mild eyes.

I have fallen a long way. Clouds are flowering
Blue and mystical over the face of the stars
Inside the church, the saints will all be blue,
Floating on their delicate feet over the cold pews.
Their hands and faces stiff with holiness.
The moon sees nothing of this. She is bald and wild.
And the message of the yew tree is blackness – blackness and silence.

SYLVIA PLATH (1932–1963)

The Worshipful Company of Moonwatchers

Among moon gazers there may be one
Who has disappeared from among us under years of sense and sanity,
Joined those who sleep behind curtains, drawn so thick
No light will wake him until the hour he appointed.
His evenings are spent on what he planned to do;
His early mornings are preparation for the day.

And then, after an illness perhaps, he is back
As surprised as we are each time, when, after an absence –
An interval when we are wrapped in our other lives –
We are surprised by the moon. He is back
Moon-watching again; gets up in the night, goes to the window
And sees the effects of a great wind roaring
Rushing like a tide through the belt of trees,
Tossing the ship of cloud bearing the effulgence
Which shows the violent busyness of this high world,
The life his sleeping household, dreaming children
And the street and whole town of safe, shut little houses
Are oblivious to.

Now once again he is out under the moon,
After the ghostly galleons of all our childhoods
The betrayed lover's moon we have crooned and sighed to
The hunter's, bomber's moon enabling death
The harvest moon that made night day for the farmers
And ended entangled in a hawthorn hedge
Like a huge football we could run to and touch.
He has gone down into the strange night garden
To watch her travel, her woe-begone face
Shifting behind the contrary wisps of clouds;
And it is as though all these moons are there:
The moon becalmed among flocked clouds,
Then suddenly reigning alone in an empty deep sky.
The moon glittering on the sea, lands away,
The little moon as frail as arrowed plane tracks
Dissolving in a summer dawn.
The blue cold wash off sterile mountains, the malign overseer
Of night fevers, peers into his dreams,
Something is there
Behind his shoulder, outside the window, at the back of the door.
He knows he has been pulled into the moon's orbit, into her circle,
That he is in that air other than
The air of day.

The realm of faery, it was one time called
Where fantasy is bred, and desire shaked through the body
And the moon draws her net, pulling the tides
Of the land as she does of the sea.

JENNY JOSEPH (1932–)

Moon

Open the book of evening to the page
where the moon, always the moon, appears
between two clouds, moving so slowly that hours
will seem to have passed before you reach the next page

where the moon, no brighter, lowers a path
to lead you away from what you have known
into those places where what you have wished for happens,
its lone syllables like a sentence poised

at the edge of sense, waiting for you to say its name
once more as you lift your eyes from the page

and close the book, still feeling what it was like
to dwell in that light, that sudden paradise of sound.

MARK STRAND (1934–)

Piano

Moonlight resting on the quiet tiles like
Hands upon the long-calmed keyboard of a grand.

Beyond the rooftops, white miles
Of highway wind across the pastureland.

Across my calmly opened
Outspread breadth of heart, this song.

O note calm
As the piano key of moonlight
Sounding it is long.

Reaching far as ache can stretch
Its miles of balm.

O harmony as deep
As pain is strong.

HARRY FAINLIGHT (1935–1982)

Eclipse of the Moon

Whose shadow's that?

Who walked in the evening
at his own ghost's back?

Who trod in the circle,
left a footprint in the frozen pond?

Who looked in the mirror
and clouded the glass?

Who snatched the white moth
in his closed fist?

Who drowned
reaching for the coin?

GILLIAN CLARKE (1937–)

On the Moon

I have left my best socks on the moon
and my shoes and my timbre.

I was paddling in Mare Nectaris
and was sweetened close to the still point

of erasure, mind-blown to extinction almost,
packed tight with crazy rare air.

I had promised myself a risky paddle
singing *A whiter shade of pale* sublimely

in Fecunditatis, Marginis and Anguis
but these seas proved a toddle too far out.

I have returned home with my voice
a mere crackling of bliss, my best gaze

left watching the earth spin. Something
tide-like thunders in, like song, stinging.

DAVID HART (1940–)

Speech Balloon

The Liverpool boss was pretty chuffed with himself,
said the news report, for being so tough
when he decided to snub the obvious choice
and go instead for the goal machine.
'I'm over the moon,' they said he said.
'I'm over the moon,' he said.

The Barnsley manager was lost for words
to describe his feelings when Chelsea fell
to the Tykes. 'We played fantastic.
I never thought we'd do it again
but we did, and all I can say is
I'm over the moon,' they said he said.
'I'm over the moon,' he said.

The Hollywood mum was way beyond thrilled
according to friends, when she delivered
into the world, not one bouncing baby
but twins instead to the astonished dad.
'I'm over the moon,' they said she said.
'I'm over the moon,' she said.

Bollywood's hottest couple was proud to be blessed
by the jubilant father, the superstar.
'It's a match made in heaven,' he said to the press,
'Between two shooting stars with shining careers
and I'm over the moon, of course,' he said.
'I'm over the moon,' he said.

The Malaysian nation went mad with joy
on independence day in the fiftieth year
when a doctor-cum-part-time-model,
a local boy, went up into space in a Russian Soyuz
and in zero gravity performed his namaz.
'All of Malaysia over the moon,' they said on the news
'twenty-seven million people over the moon.'

You must have noticed, it's really quite clear, this condition
has spread, it's happening there, it's happening here,
it's happening in every corner of every country
where English is known or English is spoken.
There's no one just satisfied or mildly pleased
or chipper or chirpy, contented or cheerful,
no one glad or gratified, delighted or jubilant,
elated, ecstatic, joyful or gleeful.
All the happy people have left this world.

You won't come across them anytime soon.

And if it's happy sound-bites you're looking for
you need to look way over your head
for the words in balloons,

to the place where the cow keeps jumping
over and over
with all the footballers, team managers
and lottery winners, world superstars
and heroes and champions and legends and lovers
and proud mums and dads

and the whole of Malaysia

over the moon
over the moon
over the
over the
over the moon.

IMTIAZ DHARKER (1954–)

The Woman in the Moon

Darlings, I write to you from the moon
where I hide behind famous light.
How could you ever think it was a man up here?
A cow jumped over. The dish ran away with the spoon.

What reached me here were your prayers, griefs,
here's the craic, losses and longing, your lives
so brief, mine long, long, a talented loneliness.
I must have a thousand names for the earth, my blue vocation.

Round I go, the moon a diet of light, sliver of pear,
wedge of lemon, slice of melon, half an orange, onion;
your human music falling through space,
the childbirth song, the lover's song, the song of death.

Devoted as words to things, I stare and stare;
deserts where forests were, vanishing seas. When your night comes,
I see you staring back as though you can hear my *Darlings,*
what have you done, what have you done to the earth?

CAROL ANN DUFFY (1955–)

Moon Hymn

I will give you one glimpse
a glimpse of the moon's grievance
whose appearance is all pocks and points
that look like frost-glints

I will wave my hand to her
in her first quarter
when the whole world is against her
shadowy exposure of her centre

o the moon loves to wander
I will go clockwise and stare
when she is huge when she is half elsewhere
half naked, in struggle with the air

and growing rounder and rounder
a pert peering creature
I love her sidling and awkward
when she's not quite circular

o criminal and ingrown
skinned animal o moon
carrying inside yourself your own
death's head, your dark one

why do you chop yourself away
piece by piece, to that final trace
of an outline of ice
on a cupful of space?

ALICE OSWALD (1966–)

Prayer

Here I work in the hollow of God's hand
with Time bent round into my reach. I touch
the circle of the earth, I throw and catch
the sun and moon by turns into my mind.
I sense the length of it from end to end,
I sway me gently in my flesh and each
point of the process changes as I watch;
the flowers come, the rain follows the wind.

And all I ask is this – and you can see
how far the soul, when it goes under flesh,
is not a soul, is small and creaturish –
that every day the sun comes silently
to set my hands to work and that the moon
turns and returns to meet me when it's done.

ALICE OSWALD (1966–)

Index of Poets

Index of Titles

Index of First Lines

Contributors' Biographies

DANNIE ABSE was born in Cardiff, in 1923. His first poetic volume, *After Every Green Thing*, was published in 1949. He has been a Fellow of the Royal Society of Literature since 1983. His last poetry collection, *Running Late*, was published in 2006. His latest book, *The Presence*, a memoir of the year after his wife died, was published in 2007 and won the 2008 Wales Book of the Year Award.

MICHAEL ALEXANDER is currently Honorary Professor of English Literature at the University of St Andrews and is best known for his verse translation of *Beowulf* (Penguin, 1973; revised edition 2001).

MARIKO ARATANI is a native speaker of Japanese and has translated a number of works of Japanese poetry, particularly focusing on the work of Ono no Komachi and Izumi Shikibu, the two foremost women poets of Japan's classical period. Outside of poetry she is a weaver and a jazz pianist.

EDWIN ARNOLD (1832–1904); an English poet and journalist: he worked on the staff of the *Daily Telegraph* for more than forty years, eventually becoming editor-in-chief. He was born in Gravesend, Kent, but travelled extensively in his life, living as far afield as India and Japan. Of his many verse collections he is best known for *The Light of Asia*, his interpretation in English verse of the life and philosophy of the East.

MATTHEW ARNOLD (1822–1888); was born in Laleham-on-Thames, England; his first poetry collection, *The Strayed Reveller and Other Poems by A.*, was published in 1849; he is probably most famous for his 1867 poem 'Dover Beach'.

W. H. AUDEN (1907–1973); was an Oxford-educated poet, critic and man of letters; born in England, he became an American citizen. During his lifetime Auden published approximately four hundred poems, including a number of works now regarded as classics of the twentieth century, such as 'Lullaby', 'As I Walked Out One Evening', 'The Unknown Citizen' and 'September 1, 1939'.

WILLIAM BARNES (1801–1886); was born in Rushay, Dorset. His Dorset dialect poems, for which he is best known, were collected in three volumes: *Poems of Rural Life in the Dorset Dialect* (1844), *Hwomely Rhymes, a Second Collection of Poems in the Dorset Dialect* (1858) and *Poems of Rural Life in the Dorset Dialect. A Third Collection* (1863).

JOHN BERRYMAN (1914–1972); was born in McAlester, Oklahoma, USA, and was the author of *The Dream Songs*.

CHARLES BEST (1570–1627); is most renowned for his poem 'A Sonnet of the Moon', which appears here and was first published in *Poetical Rhapsodie* in 1608.

ELIZABETH BISHOP (1911–1979); was an American poet born in Worcester, Massachusetts. Her collection *North & South* won the Pulitzer Prize for Poetry in 1956.

ROBERT BLY was born in Minnesota in 1926, and in February 2008 he was named the state's first poet laureate. His poetry has won numerous awards including the National Book Award for his collection *The Light Around the Body*. He has published more than forty collections of poetry, edited many others and published translations of poetry and prose from many languages.

RUPERT BROOKE (1887–1915); was born in Rugby and is mainly remembered for his idealistic war sonnets, written during the First World War; his best-known poem is probably 'The Soldier'.

ROBERT BROWNING (1812–1889); was born in Camberwell, London; a master of the dramatic monologue, his poems 'My Last Duchess' and *The Ring and the Book* are often cited as some of the finest examples of the genre.

ROBERT BURNS (1759–1796); is often celebrated as Scotland's favourite son and national poet. Born in Alloway; his poem 'Auld Lang Syne' is sung across the world at the turn of the new year.

LORD BYRON (1788–1824); was a London-born romantic poet infamously labelled, by Lady Caroline Lamb, as 'Mad, bad, and dangerous to know', who died waging the Greek War of Independence in Messolonghi, Greece. His *Childe Harold's Pilgrimage* and *Don Juan* are, respectively, masterpieces of the romantic and the comic genres of poetry.

NO CH'ONMYONG (1912–1957); was born in Changyong, Korea. She is remarkable in that her poetry is absolutely apolitical.

LING CHUNG is a Chinese scholar and poet who, along with Kenneth Rexroth, translated the *Complete Works* of the notable Sung Dynasty poet Li Ch'ing-Chao. She has also co-edited several anthologies of Chinese women poets.

JOHN CLARE (1793–1864); was born in Helpston, Northamptonshire, and is a celebrated poet of rural England. His works include *Poems Descriptive of Rural Life and Scenery* and *The Shepherd's Calendar*.

GILLIAN CLARKE was born in Cardiff, in 1937, and is a poet, playwright, editor, broadcaster, lecturer and translator (from Welsh). She has published numerous collections of poetry for adults and children, as well as dramatic commissions and articles in a wide range of publications. Her poetry is studied by GCSE and A-Level students throughout Britain. Her latest book, *At the Source*, is a journal of the writer's year.

S. T. COLERIDGE (1772–1834); one of the first English Romantic poets, was born in Devon. He is known for both his visionary poems, including *The Rime of the Ancient Mariner* and *Kubla Khan*, and his literary criticism, of which his major work is the *Biographia Literaria*.

HART CRANE (1899–1932); was born in Garrettsville, Ohio. Although his poetry is often considered difficult, his two works, *White Buildings* and *The Bridge*, have proved to be some of the most enduring of his generation.

EDWIN A. CRANSTON was born in 1932 in Pittsfield, Massachusetts. He is currently Professor of Japanese

Literature in the Faculty of Asian Languages at Harvard University. He has translated a number of Japanese works, including *The Izumi Shikibu Diary* and the poetry of Mizuno Ruriko.

ZORA CROSS (1890–1964); was born in Brisbane, Australia. As well as being a renowned novelist and journalist she wrote the seminal sonnet sequence *Songs of Love and Life*.

KEVIN CROSSLEY-HOLLAND was born in 1941 in Mursley, Buckinghamshire. Throughout his diverse career, he has been variously occupied by literature in a plethora of positions: teacher, lecturer, publisher, author (for both adults and children) and translator. In this last role, he produced seminal modern-verse translations of the Anglo Saxon poem *Beowulf*, and the Old English text commonly known as *The Exeter Book*.

E. E. CUMMINGS (1894–1962); was born in Cambridge, Massachusetts, where he remained to study at Harvard. After graduating from the university magna cum laude, he went on to write over two thousand poems, as well as producing various other literary and artistic works, for which he received numerous awards, including a Guggenheim Fellowship.

IMTIAZ DHARKER was born in 1954 in Pakistan, raised in Glasgow, and now lives between London and Mumbai. She works as a documentary film-maker in India, and is also an artist, having shown solo exhibitions in the UK, India and Hong Kong. She is the author of four poetry collections, most recently, in 2006, *The terrorist at my table*.

EMILY DICKINSON (1830–1886); was an American poet born in Amherst, Massachusetts. Dickinson was a prolific private poet: fewer than a dozen of her nearly eighteen hundred poems were published during her lifetime. It was not until after her death – when her younger sister discovered her cache of poems – that the breadth of her work became apparent.

HARRY FAINLIGHT (1935–1982); was a lover of poetry from early in his life; educated at English grammar schools and Cambridge University, where he was contemporary with Ted Hughes, it was his dual citizenship – which gave him the opportunity to travel freely to the US and view such heroes as Allen Ginsberg at first-hand – that marks his poetry most significantly.

RUTH FAINLIGHT was born in New York City in 1931. She is a poet, short-story writer, translator and librettist. Her latest collection of poetry, *Moon Wheels*, was published by Bloodaxe Books in 2006. In 2007, she was elected as a Fellow of the Royal Society of Literature.

PADRAIC FALLON (1905–1974); was an Irish poet born in Athenry, County Galway. For almost twenty-five years he served as a Customs and Excise official in County Wexford, where he lived and farmed with his wife and sons. His first book, *Poems*, appeared in 1974, the year he died.

JOHN FREEMAN (1880–1929); was born in London and was a successful English poet and essayist. He won the Hawthornden Prize in 1920 with his collection *Poems 1909–1920*.

ROBERT FROST (1874–1963); was an American poet born in San Francisco, California. He is highly regarded for his realistic depictions of rural life and his command of American colloquial speech. Honoured frequently during his lifetime, he received the Pulitzer Prize for Poetry four times.

FEDERICO GARCÍA LORCA (1898–1936); was a Spanish poet, dramatist and theatre director. An emblematic member of the 'Generation of '27'; his disappearance, at the beginning of the Spanish Civil War, is often interpreted as murder.

ROBERT GRAVES (1895–1985); was a highly prodigious English novelist, poet and translator, born in Wimbledon, London. His most commercially successful works were *I, Claudius* and *Claudius the God*, for which he was awarded the 1934 James Tait Black Memorial Prize.

EAMON GRENNAN was the Dexter M. Ferry Jr. Professor of English at Vassar College until his retirement in 2004. Born in Dublin, Ireland in 1941; his collection *Leopardi: Selected Poems* won the 1997 PEN Award for Poetry in Translation. As well as a number of Pushcart Prizes, he has also received awards from the National Endowment for the Arts, the National Endowment for the Humanities and the Guggenheim Foundation.

THOMAS HARDY (1840–1928); was born in Dorset and is one of England's most renowned novelists and poets. His work includes the novels *Jude the Obscure*, *Tess of the d'Urbervilles* and *Far From the Madding Crowd* and the poetry collections *Wessex Poems*, *Poems of the Past and Present* and *Time's Laughingstocks and Other Verses*. He was awarded the Order of Merit in 1910 for his outstanding contribution to British literature.

DAVID HART was born in 1940, and grew up in Aberystwyth. He has lived and worked in Birmingham for most of his life. He has won several major prizes, including the National Poetry Competition in 1994. He is presently part-time Honorary Teaching Fellow, University of Warwick and Lecturer in Lifelong Learning, University of Birmingham. His latest collection of verse, *Running out*, was published in 2006.

ROBERT HERRICK (1591–1674); was an English metaphysical poet born in Cheapside, London. His best-known work is the collection of lyric verse titled *Hesperides*.

JANE HIRSHFIELD was born in New York City, in 1953. She is a prize-winning poet, translator and essayist. In 2004, she was awarded the 70th Academy Fellowship for distinguished poetic achievement by the Academy of American Poets.

GERARD MANLEY HOPKINS (1844–1889); was an English poet, Roman Catholic convert and Jesuit priest. He is best known for his experimental explorations in verse meter and especially for his innovations in what he called 'sprung rhythm'.

A. E. HOUSMAN (1859–1936); was born in Bromsgrove, Worcestershire. Although best known for his cycle of poems *A Shropshire Lad*, Housman was also counted one of the foremost classicists of his age, and his editions of Juvenal, Manilius and Lucan are still considered authoritative.

TED HUGHES (1930–1998); was an English poet and children's author, born in Mytholmroyd, West Yorkshire. He was the British Poet Laureate from 1984 until his death and was awarded the Order of Merit, for his services to literature, in 1998.

T. E. HULME (1883–1917); was born in Endon, Staffordshire, and was an English poet, essayist and man of letters. His criticism and aesthetic theory were hugely influential in the formation of modernism.

ROBINSON JEFFERS (1887–1962); was born in Allegheny, Pennsylvania. The focus of his work is predominantly split between the environment, and in particular the Californian coastline where he lived, and epic verse narratives, such as *Tamar*.

ELIZABETH JENNINGS (1926–2001); was born in Boston, Lincolnshire, but moved to Oxford at the age of six, where she lived for the rest of her life. Her consistent devotion to poetry yielded over twenty books during her lifetime and amongst the many honours awarded to her are the W.H. Smith Literary Award, the Somerset Maugham Award and, in 1992, the CBE.

BEN JONSON (c.1572–1637); was born in Westminster, London, and was a contemporary, and at times a rival, of Shakespeare. Although best known for his satirical plays, which include *Volpone*, *The Alchemist* and *Bartholomew Fair*, his lyric poetry is also of exceptional quality.

JENNY JOSEPH was born in Birmingham, in 1932, and is most famous for her poem 'Warning', which was identified as the UK's 'most popular post-war poem' in a 1996 survey by the BBC. She has won a number of awards for her work, including the 1986 James Tait Black Memorial Prize, and in 1999 she became a Fellow of the Royal Society of Literature.

KOJIJU (1121–1201); was a Japanese poet, reputed to be the most beautiful, smart and independent lady in the court at the time. She left many excellent poems of passion and was rumoured to be at the centre of an amorous battle between Hei-ke and Genji.

JULES LAFORGUE (1860–1887); was born in Montevideo, Uruguay, and was a French symbolist poet, master of lyrical irony and one of the first and foremost practitioners of free verse.

PHILIP LARKIN (1922–1985); was born in Coventry and is widely considered to be one of the greatest English poets of the latter half of the twentieth century, despite only publishing four collections of verse in his lifetime: *The North Ship*, *The Less Deceived*, *The Whitsun Weddings* and *High Windows*. He received numerous awards for his verse including the Queen's Gold Medal for Poetry and, in 1975, the CBE.

D. H. LAWRENCE (1885–1930); was born in the mining town of Eastwood, Nottinghamshire, and became one of England's foremost men of letters. Over the course of his career he produced novels, plays, poetry, essays and various other forms of criticism. He is perhaps best known for his 1928 novel, *Lady Chatterley's Lover*.

EDWARD LEAR (1812–1888); was an English artist, illustrator, author and poet, renowned for his literary nonsense, in poetry and prose, and especially his limericks. In 1846 he published *A Book of Nonsense*, and in 1867 he published his most famous work, 'The Owl and the Pussycat'.

WILLIAM ELLERY LEONARD (1876–1944); was an American poet and literary scholar born in Plainfield, New Jersey. He is most remembered for *Two Lives*, a cycle of two hundred and fifty sonnets telling the story of his tragic marriage. From 1906 until the end of his life, Leonard taught at the University of Wisconsin-Madison.

GIACOMO LEOPARDI (1798–1837); was born in Recanati, Italy, and was, by all accounts, a child prodigy. Taking his education into his own hands at the age of twelve, he studied furiously for seven years, completely unsupervised, and began to produce a large volume of poems, essays and philosophical work. Sadly he realized that he had allowed his youth to pass, that henceforth his life could be only unhappy, and that above all, he would probably never be loved by a woman.

DENISE LEVERTOV (1923–1997); was born in Ilford, Essex. She wrote and published more than twenty books of poetry, criticism and translations. Among her many awards and honours, she received the Shelley Memorial Award, the Robert Frost Medal, the Lenore Marshall Prize, the Lannan Award and a Guggenheim Fellowship.

PHILIP LEVINE is a Pulitzer Prize-winning American poet. He was born in Detroit, Michigan, in 1928, and is currently a Distinguished Poet in Residence for the creative-writing programme at New York University. Amongst his awards are the National Book Award, two National Book Critics Circle Awards, the American Book Award for Poetry, the Frank O'Hara Prize and two Guggenheim Fellowships.

AMY LOWELL (1874–1925); was an American poet born in Brookline, Massachusetts. She was posthumously awarded the 1926 Pulitzer Prize for Poetry for her final collection of verse, *What's O'Clock*, published in 1925.

LU YU (1125 –1209); was born on a boat floating in the Wei Water River and was a Chinese poet of the southern Song dynasty. Amazingly, he wrote more than ten thousand poems in his life and more than nine thousand examples of his verse survive.

WILLIAM McGONAGALL (1825–1902); was an Edinburgh-born weaver, actor and poet. His critical reception has been hugely mixed: some consider him one of the worst poets in the English language, whilst others believe that his use of unusual metaphors and clunking rhythms make his some of the most amusing in all of British comic verse.

ARCHIBALD MacLEISH (1892–1982); was an American writer, born in Glencoe, Illinois; he won the Pulitzer Prize three times in his life, twice for poetry and once for drama. His *Collected Poems 1917–1952* also won the National Book Award in 1933 and his play, *J.B.*, won a Tony Award for Best Play in 1959. He was the Librarian of Congress from 1939 to 1944.

P. E. MATHESON (1859–1946); was a British man of letters at Oxford University. An honorary Fellow of New College, he was of particular renown in the field of Roman history.

EDNA ST VINCENT MILLAY (1892–1950); was an American poet and playwright (although she also penned prose work under the name of Nancy Boyd) born in Rockland, Maine. In 1923 she became the first woman to receive the Pulitzer Prize for Poetry, and in 1943 she was awarded the Frost Medal for her lifetime contribution to American verse.

JOHN MILTON (1608–1674); was born in Cheapside, London, and was an English poet, author, polemicist and civil servant for the Commonwealth of England. He is best known for his epic poem *Paradise Lost*, which deals with the story of the Fall of Man; the temptation of Adam and Eve by Satan and the events in the garden leading up to their expulsion from Eden.

HAROLD MONRO (1879–1932); was a British poet born in Brussels, Belgium. As well as writing verse he founded a highly influential poetry magazine, *The Poetry Review*, and he followed this, in 1912, by founding the Poetry Bookshop in Bloomsbury, London.

THOMAS MOORE (1779–1852); was an entertainer, poet, singer and songwriter born in Dublin, Ireland. He is so widely revered in Ireland that he is considered to be the national bard.

EDWIN MORGAN is a Scottish poet and translator born in Glasgow in 1920. In 1999 he was declared Glasgow's first Poet Laureate and in 2004 he was named as the first Scottish national poet. Among his awards and honours are the Queen's Gold Medal for Poetry, the Weidenfeld Prize for Translation and the OBE.

NIKOLAY PLATONOVICH OGAREV (1813–1877); was a Russian poet, historian and political activist. He is perhaps best know as the fellow-exile and collaborator of Alexander Herzen on *Kolokol*, a revolutionary newspaper printed in England and smuggled into Russia.

KEVIN O'ROURKE was born in 1939 and is currently Professor of English Literature in Kyung Hee University, Seoul. A distinguished Korean studies specialist and translator, he is the author of over twenty books on Korean literature and numerous verse translations into English.

ALICE OSWALD was born in 1966. Her collection of poetry *The Thing in the Gap-Stone Stile*, won a Forward Poetry Prize for Best First Collection in 1996. Her second collection, *Dart*, won the T. S. Eliot Prize in 2002. Her latest collection, *Woods etc.*, was published in 2005 and was shortlisted for the Forward Prize for Best Collection of the Year.

RUTH PITTER (1897–1992); was a renowned poet born in Ilford, Essex. In 1955 she became the first woman to receive the Queen's Gold Medal for Poetry. She was appointed CBE in 1979; in 1974 she was named a Companion of Literature, the highest honour given by the Royal Society of Literature.

SYLVIA PLATH (1932–1963); was an American poet and author, born in Jamaica Plain, Massachusetts.

She is considered one of the twentieth century's most distinctive voices and in 1982 she won the Pulitzer Prize for *The Collected Poems*. Although she is known primarily for her poetry, her novel, *The Bell Jar*, is also considered a modern classic.

KENNETH REXROTH (1905–1982); was an American poet, translator and critical essayist born in South Bend, Indiana. Heavily involved in the San Francisco Renaissance of the mid-twentieth century, he is hailed by many as 'the father of the Beats'; to honour his contribution, a street in the city now bears his name.

EDWIN ARLINGTON ROBINSON (1869 –1935); was born in Maine and published his first collection, *The Torrent and the Night Before*, in 1896. He won the Pulitzer Prize for Poetry three times, in 1922, 1925 and 1928.

CHRISTINA ROSSETTI (1830–1894); was a British poet who, like her brother Dante, was born London. She is best known for her long poem *Goblin Market*, her love poem 'Remember' and for her Christmas poem 'In the Bleak Midwinter'.

DANTE GABRIEL ROSSETTI (1828–1882); was born in London, England. As well as writing poetry he was integral to the founding of the Pre-Raphaelite movement in painting.

VITA SACKVILLE-WEST (1892–1962); was an author and poet, famous for her exuberant lifestyle, born at the venerable Knole House in Kent. Her long narrative poem, *The Land*, won the Hawthornden Prize in

1927. She won it again, becoming the only writer to do so, in 1933 with her *Collected Poems*.

SAPPHO (c. 610–570 BC); was a famed female Greek poet born at Eresos on the island of Lesbos. She is said to be the first published female poet. Although almost two hundred fragments of her poetry are extant many of these are only a word or a phrase.

SIEGFRIED SASSOON (1886–1967); was born in Matfield, Kent, and was a writer and poet in the early twentieth century. During the First World War he wrote satirical anti-war poetry and also a number of polemical prose works. He is now best known for his works of fictionalized autobiography, linked by their central protagonist George Sherston.

ROBERT SERVICE (1874–1958); was born to Scottish parents in Preston, Lancashire. He was a poet and writer famed for his works on the Canadian North, which include 'The Shooting of Dan McGrew', 'The Law of the Yukon' and 'The Cremation of Sam McGee'. His writing was so expressive that he has often been informally labelled as 'the Bard of the Yukon' and he was honoured on a Canadian postage stamp in 1976.

VIKRAM SETH was born in Calcutta, India, in 1952. He has written works in a variety of forms, including poetry, narrative prose fiction and memoir, across myriad literary genres. His familiarity with a wide range of languages and his placement at a confluence of cultures has ensured that his work is varied and sometimes controversial. Currently, he is believed to be working on *A Suitable Girl*, which he called a 'jump sequel', to his 1993 novel, *A Suitable Boy*.

PERCY BYSSHE SHELLEY (1792–1822); was an English Romantic poet, and a contemporary of Keats and Byron, born in Horsham, England. He is equally renowned for his visionary, revolutionary works, such as *The Revolt of Islam* and *Prometheus Unbound*, and for his lyric verse, which includes the oft-anthologized 'To a Skylark', 'Ozymandias' and 'Ode to the West Wind'.

LADY IZUMI SHIKIBU (c. 970–1030); was one of the towering figures of Japanese literature. The daughter of a Japanese provincial governor, she lived in Kyoto and began service at court in her early teens. She became an official companion to the Empress, and in 995 was married to the Governor of Izumi. Some years later, she scandalized the court by abandoning her husband to become the lover of one of the Empress's sons.

SIR PHILIP SIDNEY (1554–1586); was an Elizabethan courtier, soldier, writer and poet born in Penshurst, Kent. His major works of prose are *The Defence of Poetry* and the romantic pastoral narrative *The Countess of Pembroke's Arcadia*. He also wrote many celebrated poems including his sonnet sequence, *Astrophel and Stella*.

CHARLOTTE SMITH (1749–1806); was an English poet and novelist. Her poetry was revered by her contemporaries – William Wordsworth, in particular, was a vociferous supporter of her verse. Her collection *Elegiac Sonnets* is often credited with inspiring a revival of the sonnet form in English; other works include *The Emigrants* and the posthumous collection, *Beachy Head and Other Poems*.

WILLIAM JAY SMITH was born in 1918 in Winnfield, Louisiana, and is currently Professor Emeritus of English Literature at Hollins University. He served as Consultant in Poetry to the Library of Congress from 1968 to 1970 and is the author of ten collections of poetry of which two were finalists for the National Book Award. He has been member of the American Academy of Arts and Letters since 1975.

EDMUND SPENSER (c. 1552–1599); born in London, Spenser was an Elizabethan poet and courtier. His long, unfinished work, *The Faerie Queene*, is a dense and fantastical allegory dealing with the history of the Tudor dynasty and the Church in England. The verse form of the poem was so distinctive that it is now commonly know as Spenserian stanza.

MARK STRAND was born in Summerside, Canada, in 1934 and he has been a Professor of English at Columbia University since 2005. In 1981, he was elected a member of the American Academy of Arts and Letters and he served as Poet Laureate Consultant in Poetry to the Library of Congress during the 1990–1991 term. He has received numerous awards for his poetry including a MacArthur Fellowship, in 1987, and the Pulitzer Prize for Poetry, in 1999, for his collection *Blizzard of One*.

SU TUNG-P'O (1036 –1101); was a Chinese poet born in the present-day Sichuan province. He was one of a literary family and occupied many official posts, rising to President of the Board of Rites, although his satiric verses and opposition to official policies frequently lost him his official status. Su's poetry and art were inspired by Taoism and Buddhism, although his political views were founded in Confucian philosophy. Su is generally considered the greatest poet of the Sung dynasty.

MAY SWENSON (1913–1989); was a poet and playwright born in Logan, Utah. She was involved in poetry throughout her life and held a number of related positions: as poet-in-residence at a number of universities; from 1959 to 1966, as an editor at New Directions publishers; and from 1980 until her death in 1989, as a Chancellor of the Academy of American Poets.

ARTHUR SYMONS (1865–1945); was born in Wales and was a poet, playwright, translator, critic and magazine editor. His first volume of verse, published in 1889, was titled *Days and Nights*. Probably his single most important work is his prose volume *The Symbolist Movement in Literature*, which had a major influence on both W. B. Yeats and T. S. Eliot.

SARA TEASDALE (1884–1933); was an American lyric poet born in St Louis, Missouri. In 1918 she won the Pulitzer Prize for Poetry with her collection *Love Songs*.

CHARLES TENNYSON TURNER (1808–1879); was an English poet born in Somersby, Lincolnshire. He was the elder brother of the nineteenth-century British poet laureate Alfred Tennyson, a relationship which was celebrated in the collection *Poems by Two Brothers*.

DYLAN THOMAS (1914–1953); although born in Swansea, Wales, he wrote his poetry exclusively in English. He is perhaps most famous for his villanelle, 'Do not go gentle into that good night', and his play, *Under Milk Wood*.

EDWARD THOMAS (1878–1917); was born in Lambeth, London. Astonishingly, he wrote a lifetime's poetry in two years. Already a dedicated prose writer and influential critic, he became a poet only in December 1914, at the age of thirty-six. In April 1917 he was killed in the First World War.

R. S. THOMAS (1913–2000); was a Cardiff-born poet and Anglican clergyman. After the publication of his fourth collection, *Song at the Year's Turning*, by a major publisher, he became one of the most famous Welsh poets of the twentieth century. Such is his significance that in 1996 he was nominated for the Nobel Prize for Literature, although he lost to Seamus Heaney.

TU FU (712–770); born in the modern-day Henan province of China, he was a prominent poet of the Tang Dynasty. Unusually there are nearly fifteen hundred preserved examples of his verse.

PAUL VERLAINE (1844–1896); was a French poet associated with both the Symbolist movement and the *fin de siècle*. His first collection, *Poèmes saturniens*, published in 1866, won him acclaim for his promise and originality. He was born in Metz.

HELEN WADDELL (1889–1965); was an Irish poet, translator and playwright born in Tokyo, Japan. In addition to her verse, she also wrote a historical novel, *Peter Abelard*. She was the first woman to be awarded the Benson Medal, founded in 1916, to honour those who produce 'meritorious works in poetry, fiction, history and belles-lettres', by the Royal Society of Literature.

ARTHUR WALEY (1889–1966); was a renowned poet, translator, orientalist and sinologist born in London. So great was his contribution to literature that in 1945 he was awarded an honorary Fellowship of King's College, Cambridge; in 1952, he was appointed CBE; in 1953, he won the Queen's Gold Medal for Poetry; and in 1956, he was awarded membership of the Order of the Companions of Honour.

WALT WHITMAN (1819–1892); was born on Long Island in New York and was a celebrated American poet, essayist and journalist. His collection *Leaves of Grass* is arguably the single best-known collection of American poetry.

ELINOR WYLIE (1885–1928); was an American poet and novelist born in Somerville, New Jersey. Her poetry collections include *Black Armour* (1923), *Trivial Breath* (1928) and *Angels and Earthly Creatures* (1929).

YANG-TI (569–618), was the son and heir of Emperor Wen of Sui. He ascended the throne in 604 and ruled, as the third Emperor of China's Sui Dynasty, until 617.

W. B. YEATS (1865–1939); was born in Dublin, Ireland, and was one of the foremost figures of twentieth-century letters. Yeats wrote countless poems, plays and works of criticism spanning a fifty-year period; his range and consistent brilliance were celebrated internationally when, in 1923, he was awarded the Nobel Prize for Literature.

YI KYUBO (1168–1241); was a Korean poet who had a long and distinguished public career, which culminated in his appointment as head of the Chancellery of State Affairs. Currently, there are more than two thousand poems to his credit, including the celebrated epic *The Lay of King Tongmyong*.

YU HSUAN-CHI (843–868); was born in Chang'an, China, during the Tang Dynasty. She is distinctive for being the first Chinese poet to break the conventional passive voice of women in Chinese poetry. In her lifetime, her verse was published in a now lost collection, *Fragments of a Northern Dreamland*.

Acknowledgements

The editor and the publishers wish to thank the following for permission to use copyright material:

JEANNE THOMAS ALLEN – Excerpt from *Now, Voyager* by Jeanne Thomas Allen © 1984 by the Board of Regents of the University of Wisconsin System. Reprinted by permission of Wisconsin Press.

HELEN WADDELL, translator – 'The Morning Glory', by The Shi King, translated by Helen Waddell. Translation copyright © Helen Waddell. Reprinted by kind permission of Louise Anson.

ARTHUR WALEY, translator – 'Flowers and Moonlight on the Spring River', by Yang-Ti, translated by Arthur Waley from *Chinese Poems* (George Allen & Unwin Ltd., 1946). Translation copyright © The Arthur Waley Estate. Reprinted by kind permission of The Arthur Waley Estate.

KENNETH REXROTH, translator – 'Full Moon' and 'Night Thoughts' by Kenneth Rexroth, from the original by Lu Yu, from *One Hundred Poems From The Chinese*, copyright © 1971 by Kenneth Rexroth. Reprinted by permission of New Directions Publishing Corp.

'Living in the Summer Mountains' by Kenneth Rexroth, from the original by Yu Hsuan-Chi, from *Women Poets of China*, copyright © 1973 by Kenneth Rexroth and Ling Chung. Reprinted by permission of New Directions Publishing Corp.

'Moon, Flowers, Man' by Kenneth Rexroth, from the original by Su Tung P'o, from *One Hundred Poems From The Chinese*, copyright © 1971 by Kenneth Rexroth. Reprinted by permission of New Directions Publishing Corp.

VIKRAM SETH, translator – 'Moonlit Night', by Tu Fu, translated by Vikram Seth from *Three Chinese Poets* (Harper Perennial, 1993). Translation copyright © Vikram Seth, 1993. Reprinted by kind permission of David Godwin Associates Ltd. on behalf of Vikram Seth.

MICHAEL ALEXANDER, translator – 'Riddle', from *The Earliest English Poems* translated and introduced by Michael Alexander (Penguin Classics 1966, third edition 1991). Copyright © Michael Alexander 1966, 1977, 1991.

KEVIN CROSSLEY-HOLLAND, translator – 'Riddle', translated by Kevin Crossley-Holland, from *The Exeter Book Riddles* Revised Ed., trans. Kevin Crossley-Holland (Enitharmon Press, 2008). Translation copyright © 1993, 2008 by Kevin Crossley-Holland. Reprinted with the kind permission of Enitharmon Press.

KEVIN O'ROURKE, translator – 'Evening on the mountain song to the moon in the well', by Yi Kyubo, translated by Kevin O'Rourke, from *Tilting the jar, spilling the moon*. Copyright © Kevin O'Rourke. Used with the permission of The Dedalus Press, www.dedaluspress.com.

JULES LAFORGUE – 'Clair de Lune', by Jules Laforgue, translated by William Jay Smith, from *Collected Translations*. Translation copyright © 1985 by William Jay Smith. Reprinted with the permission of New Rivers Press, www.newriverspress.com.

W. B. YEATS – 'The Cat and the Moon', by W. B. Yeats from *The Wild Swans at Coole* (Macmillan, London, 1919). Copyright © 1919 W. B. Yeats. Reproduced with the kind permission of A. P. Watt Ltd. (Literary Agents), on behalf of Gráinne Yeats.

SIEGFRIED SASSOON – 'A Poplar and the Moon', by Siegfried Sassoon. Copyright © Siegfried Sassoon. Reprinted by kind permission of the Estate of George Sassoon.

ROBINSON JEFFERS – 'Hooded Night', by Robinson Jeffers from *The Collected Poetry of Robinson Jeffers*, edited by Tim Hunt. Copyright © 1938 and 1966 by Donnan and Garth Jeffers. All rights reserved. Used with the permission of Stanford University Press, www.sup.org.

VITA SACKVILLE-WEST – 'Full Moon', by Vita Sackville-West reproduced with permission of Curtis Brown Group Ltd., London on behalf of the Estate of Vita Sackville-West. Copyright © Vita Sackville-West 1933.

ARCHIBALD MACLEISH – 'Ars Poetica', by Archibald MacLeish from *Collected Poems 1917–1982* by Archibald MacLeish. Copyright © 1985 by The Estate of Archibald MacLeish. Reprinted by permission of Houghton Mifflin Harcourt Publishing Company. All rights reserved.

E. E. CUMMINGS – 'who knows if the moon's', by E. E. Cummings is reprinted from *Complete Poems 1904–1962*, by E. E. Cummings, edited by George J. Firmage, by permission of W. W. Norton & Company. Copyright © 1991 by the Trustees for the E. E. Cummings Trust and George James Firmage.

ROBERT GRAVES – 'The Cruel Moon', by Robert Graves, is reprinted from *Complete Poems in One Volume* edited by Beryl Graves and Dunstan Ward (Manchester, Carcanet, 2001). Reprinted by kind permission of Carcanet Press Limited.

FEDERICO GARCÍA LORCA – 'The Moon Sails Out', by Federico García Lorca, translated by Robert Bly. Translation copyright © 1973, 1997 by Robert Bly. Reprinted by permission of Georges Borchardt, Inc., for Robert Bly.

ELIZABETH BISHOP – 'Insomnia' from *The Complete Poems 1927–1979* by Elizabeth Bishop. Copyright © 1979, 1983, by Alice Helen Methfessel. Reprinted by permission of Farrar, Straus and Giroux, LLC.

DYLAN THOMAS – 'Clowns in the Moon' and 'In My Craft or Sullen Art', by Dylan Thomas are reprinted from *The Poems* edited by Daniel Jones (Dent, 1971). Reproduced with permission of David Higham Associates Limited.

JOHN BERRYMAN – 'The Moon and the Night and the Men', by John Berryman. Copyright © The Estate of John Berryman. Reprinted by kind permission of Kate Donahue.

EDWIN MORGAN – 'Translunar Space March 1972', by Edwin Morgan, is reprinted by kind permission of Carcanet Press Limited.

ELIZABETH JENNINGS – 'In Praise of Creation', by Elizabeth Jennings, is reprinted from *New Collected Poems* edited by Michael Schmidt (Carcanet, 2002). Reproduced with permission of David Higham Associates Limited.

PHILIP LEVINE – 'You can have it', from *New Selected Poems* by Philip Levine, copyright © 1991 by Philip Levine. Used by permission of Alfred A. Knopf, a division of Random House, Inc.

JENNY JOSEPH – 'The Worshipful Company of Moonwatchers', by Jenny Joseph. Copyright © Jenny Joseph 2007. Reproduced with permission of Johnson & Alcock Ltd.

MARK STRAND – 'Moon', from *Man and Camel* by Mark Strand, copyright © 2006 by Mark Strand. Used by permission of Alfred A. Knopf, a division of Random House, Inc.